Edexcel GCSE
Religious Studies

Religion and Life

Based on a Study of Christianity and Islam

Sarah K. Tyler
and Gordon Reid

Philip Allan Updates, an imprint of Hodder Education, an Hachette UK company, Market Place, Deddington, Oxfordshire OX15 0SE

Orders
Bookpoint Ltd, 130 Milton Park, Abingdon, Oxfordshire OX14 4SB
tel: 01235 827720
fax: 01235 400454
e-mail: uk.orders@bookpoint.co.uk
Lines are open 9.00 a.m.–5.00 p.m., Monday to Saturday, with a 24-hour message answering service. You can also order through the Philip Allan Updates website: www.philipallan.co.uk

© Philip Allan Updates 2009
ISBN 978-0-340-98716-2

First printed 2009
Impression number   5   4   3   2   1
Year   2014   2013   2012   2011   2010   2009

All rights reserved; no part of this publication may be reproduced, stored in a retrieval system, or transmitted, in any form or by any means, electronic, mechanical, photocopying, recording or otherwise without either the prior written permission of Philip Allan Updates or a licence permitting restricted copying in the United Kingdom issued by the Copyright Licensing Agency Ltd, Saffron House, 6–10 Kirby Street, London EC1N 8TS

Printed in Italy

Hachette UK's policy is to use papers that are natural, renewable and recyclable products and made from wood grown in sustainable forests. The logging and manufacturing processes are expected to conform to the environmental regulations of the country of origin.

Contents

About this book 5

Believing in God 7
    Topic 1   Believing in God 8
    Topic 2   Religious upbringing 10
    Topic 3   Religious experience — the numinous and conversion 12
    Topic 4   Religious experience — miracles and prayer 14
    Topic 5   The arguments from causation and design 18
    Topic 6   Scientific explanations of the origin of the world 21
    Topic 7   Christian responses to scientific explanations for the origins of the world 24
    Topic 8   Unanswered prayer 26
    Topic 9   The problem of evil and suffering 28
    Topic 10   Religious programming on television and radio 33

Matters of life and death 35
    Topic 11   Christian and Islamic beliefs about life after death 36
    Topic 12   Non-religious belief in life after death 41
    Topic 13   Abortion 44
    Topic 14   Euthanasia 50
    Topic 15   Matters of life and death in the media 55

Marriage and family 57
    Topic 16   Changing attitudes towards marriage, divorce, family and homosexuality 58
    Topic 17   Christian attitudes to sex outside marriage 61
    Topic 18   Muslim attitudes to sex outside marriage 63
    Topic 19   Christian attitudes to divorce 65
    Topic 20   Muslim attitudes to divorce 68
    Topic 21   Christian teachings on family life 70
    Topic 22   Muslim teachings on family life 73
    Topic 23   Christian attitudes to homosexuality 75
    Topic 24   Muslim attitudes to homosexuality 78
    Topic 25   Christian attitudes to contraception 80
    Topic 26   Muslim attitudes to contraception 83

Religion and community cohesion 85

- **Topic 27** Changing attitudes to gender roles 86
- **Topic 28** Christian attitudes to equal rights for women 89
- **Topic 29** Muslim attitudes towards equal rights for women 92
- **Topic 30** The UK as a multi-ethnic society 96
- **Topic 31** Government action to promote community cohesion 99
- **Topic 32** Why Christians should promote racial harmony 102
- **Topic 33** Why Muslims should promote racial harmony 105
- **Topic 34** The UK as a multi-faith society 108
- **Topic 35** Issues raised about multi-faith societies 112
- **Topic 36** Ways in which religions work to promote community cohesion .. 116
- **Topic 37** Issues of religion and community cohesion in the media 120

Key word index 123

About this book

This book is intended to help you revise for your GCSE in religious studies. It covers the material relevant to the Edexcel Religion and Life unit, focusing on Christianity and Islam. If you are studying Religion and Life Christianity only, or Christianity with another religion, this book still contains much of the information you need to revise.

Revision suggests that you have already covered the course in some detail, so you are advised to use this book after you have studied each topic area in class and are already quite confident with the material. The book will help fill any gaps and remind you of the key information you need for the exam, but there is always room for you to add further information you have learned from classes or your own work.

Your aim is to arrive in the exam room equipped with the knowledge and skills to do well in the exam. The knowledge will be provided by your teacher and whatever course books you use, but you have to memorise it yourself, and you have to know how best to apply it. Most questions on the paper will be familiar in their structure and demands and you are likely to have answered them before for homework or mock exams. You will know that there will be questions worth 2 marks asking you to give definitions of terms, questions worth 6 marks and 8 marks asking you to explain reasons why certain beliefs are held and a further question worth 6 marks that asks for your opinion on a matter of belief and practice as well as the views of others. You will never be asked about something that is not on the specification and there will never be a question that does not follow the format.

The key to doing well in your exam is not to know obscure information, or to be able to write far more than anyone else. The key is simply to know what the examiner expects you to know — the core information and arguments about the topics you have studied. If you know these well and are ready in the exam to express them clearly and concisely, doing exactly what the question asks of you, then you can do well.

This book can help you by:
- providing a summary of the key information for each area you study
- identifying key works and their meanings
- providing test questions and exercises to help consolidate the material
- including simple exam-style questions so you can practise following the format by which you communicate what you have learned, and work to time long before you enter the exam room
- providing a list of all the key words and the pages on which they appear (see page 123)

Exam questions will always use the same command or trigger words. Look at page 17 to see this for yourself:

- Question (a) will always include the phrase 'What is meant...'
- Question (b) will always ask 'Do you think...?'
- Question (c) will always ask 'Why do some people...?'
- Question (d) will always include a trigger statement and ask 'Do you agree? Give reasons for your view' and 'Give reasons why some people may disagree with you.'

Revision rules

- Start early.
- Plan your time by making a timetable.
- Be realistic — don't try to do too much each night.
- Find somewhere quiet to work.
- Revise thoroughly including learning the set texts — reading on its own is not enough.
- Summarise your notes, make headings for each topic.
- Ask someone to test you.
- Try to answer some questions from old papers. Your teacher will help you.

If there is anything you don't understand — ask your teacher.

Be prepared

The night before the exam
- Complete your final revision.
- Check the time and place of your examination.
- Get your pens ready.
- Go to bed early and set the alarm clock.

On the examination day
- Don't rush.
- Double check the time and place of your exam and your equipment.
- Arrive early.
- Keep calm — breathe deeply.
- Be positive.

Do you know?

- The exam board setting your paper?
- How many papers you will be taking?
- The date, time and place of each paper?
- How long each paper will be?
- What the subject of each paper will be?
- What the paper will look like? Do you write your answer on the paper or in a separate booklet?
- How many questions you should answer?
- Whether there is a choice of questions?
- Whether any part of the paper is compulsory?

If you don't know the answer to any of these questions as the exam approaches — ask your teacher.

Examination tips

- Keep calm and concentrate.
- Read the paper through before you start to write.
- In Part B, decide which question you are going to answer.
- Make sure you can do all parts of the questions you choose.
- Complete all the questions.
- Don't spend too long on one question at the expense of the others.
- Read each question carefully, then stick to the point and answer questions fully.
- In evaluation questions, include Christian teaching and more than one viewpoint.
- Use all your time.
- Check your answers.
- Do your best.

Believing in God

(This module is always from the perspective of Christianity only)

Topic 1
Believing in God

People who believe in the existence of God are likely to have come to that belief through one or more of a number of possible ways. Individuals have their own story to tell about why they believe in God. Similarly, those who don't believe in God will do so for many reasons.

A believer in God is called a **theist**. Theists are likely to believe that:
- God created the world
- people can have a personal relationship with God
- God answers prayers and may perform miracles
- God is **omnipotent** (all powerful), **omniscient** (all knowing) and **omni-benevolent** (all good and all loving)
- belief in God gives meaning to life and its difficulties
- the fact that so many people believe in God goes some way to proving that he must exist

An **atheist** is someone who does not believe in the existence of God. People may be atheists because:
- they have grown up without learning about God
- they have not been given a good reason to believe in God
- they object to the way religion teaches people about the world and how to live

An **agnostic** is someone who believes that it is impossible to know whether or not God exists.

Exam tip
Make sure that you can offer good reasons why all these examples could be challenged by atheists as well as by some Christians who do not share these experiences of God.

Some atheists describe themselves as **antitheists**. An antitheist strongly objects to religious belief, and may claim that it is wrong or dangerous.

Richard Dawkins is a well-known antitheist

> **Key words**
>
> **Agnostic** — a person who claims that we cannot know whether God exists
>
> **Antitheist** — a person who is opposed to religious belief
>
> **Atheist** — a person who rejects belief in the existence of God
>
> **Omni-benevolent** — all loving and all good
>
> **Omnipotent** — all powerful
>
> **Omniscient** — all knowing
>
> **Theist** — a person who believes in God

Test yourself

1. Explain the meaning of the following terms:
   - omnipotent
   - omni-benevolent
   - atheist

2. How do you think the following quotations from the Bible express a Christian belief in God?
   - 'In the beginning God created the heavens and the earth' (Genesis 1:1).
   - 'So God created humankind in his own image' (Genesis 1:27).
   - 'You shall have no other Gods before me' (Exodus 20:3).

3. What are the main differences between an atheist, an antitheist and an agnostic?

Examination question

a **What is meant by omniscient?** (2 marks)

b **What is an agnostic?** (2 marks)

c **Do you think there are good reasons to believe in God? Give two reasons for your view.** (6 marks)

d **Why do some people believe in God and some others are atheist?** (8 marks)

Topic 2
Religious upbringing

For a good number of religious believers, their faith is closely associated with the beliefs their parents and extended family hold, and family life is bound together by that faith. Shared belief between family members and members of the community is seen to be very important in preserving belief in God and maintaining the importance of religion for generations to come. Families and communities are unified by their shared faith and practices, which may give them a special identity, and their belief in God can be supported by:

- **praying** and worshipping together and with other members of their faith
- witnessing to other communities or individuals (telling them about their faith, through personal **testimony**)
- taking care of each other and encouraging one another in difficult times.
- celebrating religious festivals and sacraments (such as **confirmation**)
- rejoicing together and thanking God for good things

Christian families are likely to:
- introduce children to the faith through the **initiation ceremony** of **baptism**
- encourage them to attend Sunday school and church
- worship together as a family
- share their life and their faith with the rest of their religious community

One of the main purposes of marriage is to have children and to bring them up in a secure and loving Christian family and the **Bible** offers guidance on family relationships.
- Exodus 20:12 says 'Honour your father and your mother'.
- Ephesians 6:1 teaches children to 'Obey your parents...for this is right'.
- Ephesians 6:4 also teaches parents not to make their children angry.

Some Christian families adopt strict principles of biblical parenting for their children based on Proverbs 22:6: 'Train children in the right way, and when old, they will not stray'.

Key words

Baptism — the Christian rite of initiation that welcomes a person into the Christian community

Bible — the sacred text of Christianity

Confirmation — where young Christians make the baptismal vows for themselves

Initiation ceremony — a ritual, such as baptism, that makes a person a member of a new community or group that holds a set of beliefs in common

Prayer — communicating with God through words or meditation, alone or with others

Testimony — a public statement of faith and belief

Biblical parenting may include home schooling — teaching children the full academic curriculum at home rather than at school — strict rules on dating and socialising, limitations on television, films and the internet, and even disciplining their children in a godly way, which may include appropriate physical punishments. This is a controversial approach to religious upbringing, and there are many websites that explain more about it, such as www.biblicalparenting.org.

Test yourself

1 As a class discuss these questions:
   - Is it true that a religious upbringing for a child always leads to a secure and happy adult life?
   - For what reasons may biblical parenting be a good or bad thing?
   - Have you had a religious upbringing? If so, what have been the advantages and disadvantages of it?

2 In what ways can families and the local community lead a person to belief in God?

3 'Children should always follow the beliefs of their family and community.'

'Parents should let their children decide for themselves if God exists and should not try to influence them.'

For each of these claims:
  i Do you agree? Give reasons for your view.
  ii Give reasons why some people may disagree with you.

Examination question

a **Do you think that being brought up in a Christian family is likely to lead to belief in God? Give two reasons for your view.** (6 marks)

b **Why do some people believe that a religious upbringing may not be helpful for future belief in God?** (8 marks)

c **'Women are better equipped to become priests than men.'**
  i **Do you agree? Give reasons for your view.** (3 marks)
  ii **Give reasons why some people may disagree with you.** (3 marks)

Exam tip
Knowing some Bible references to support your answers will immediately improve your mark for these questions.

Topic 3
Religious experience — the numinous and conversion

In the modern world, many people have been brought up outside a traditional religious background, and yet still find faith in God through more personal experience. Some people consider that this leads to a more genuine faith and argue that everyone must find a personal reason to believe in God independently of the faith of their parents in particular. Personal experience keeps faith alive, and many people over the centuries have claimed that vivid, personal, and direct experience of God has convinced them of his existence in a way that nothing else could. There are three special types of personal experience: *religious experience*, including **conversion**, *miracles*, and *prayer*.

Religious experience

There are many varieties of religious experience, all of which may come under the description of an encounter with God.

Mystical experiences
e.g. hearing God's voice, seeing a vision of a religious figure (perhaps Jesus or a saint), or a dream that offered divine guidance

A conversion experience
e.g. when an person is converted from one faith to another or from having no faith at all to belief in God

Encounters with God might include…

A charismatic experience
e.g. speaking in tongues, prophecy, healing or a miracle

A near death experience

One of the best known accounts is that of Saul, a highly educated and religious Jew who opposed the early Christians. His experience is described in Acts 9:4–5:

'As he neared Damascus on his journey, suddenly a light from heaven flashed around him. He fell to the ground and heard a voice say to him, "Saul, Saul, why do you persecute me?"

"Who are you, Lord?" Saul asked.

"I am Jesus, whom you are persecuting," he replied.'

God made him blind for three days, during which time he came to accept Jesus as the Messiah.

Whatever form the experiences take, the feelings they generate are perhaps the most important aspect. A religious experience is often described as being **numinous** — this describes feelings of awe (holy fear and wonder), a heightened spiritual awareness and a sense of being either very close to God or very separated from him. An increased love for God and a desire to serve him are likely to be results of a genuine religious experience.

> **Key words**
>
> **Conversion** — a change from one faith to another or from no faith to belief
>
> **Numinous** — having a feeling of awe and wonder

Test yourself

1. Explain how having a religious experience might lead someone to believe in God
2. Describe **two** different types of religious experience found in the Bible. List the key features of each one.
3. Do you think that people really have religious experiences?
4. Give an example of a charismatic experience.
5. Give an example of a mystical experience.
6. What is meant by 'numinous'?

Examination question

a. What is a conversion experience? (2 marks)

b. Do you think that religious experiences are possible? Give two reasons for your answer. (6 marks)

c. Why do some people believe that religious experiences are not genuine experiences of God? (8 marks)

d. 'If God were all loving he would give everyone religious experiences.'
   i. Do you agree? Give reasons for your view. (3 marks)
   ii. Give reasons why some people may disagree with you. (3 marks)

Exam tip

A religious experience need not be dramatic. Some Christians would interpret everyday things as a religious experience if they learned more about God through them.

Topic 4
Religious experience — miracles and prayer

Miracles

Miracles are a special category of religious experience, and are most often described as events that break a natural law. For religious believers, God is thought to be the best explanation for why such an unexpected event might take place. Someone who experiences a miracle may come to believe in God because it seems as if there is no other reason why it may have happened.

Miracles must have at least three characteristics:
- The event that takes place is against our regular experience of things.
- It has a beneficial outcome.
- It is performed by God.

Jesus was a miracle worker and in the Gospels he is described as performing many acts that could not have happened naturally. After his death and resurrection, the apostles and other members of the Early Church also performed miracles and it was clearly something that was part of their regular experience.

Read the following accounts of miracles:
- Mark 5:35–41 (the calming of the storm)
- Luke 8:40–56 (Jairus's daughter and the woman with the haemorrhage)
- Matthew 14:13–21 (the feeding of the 5,000)
- John 11:1–44 (the raising of Lazarus)
- Acts 3–10 (the healing of the crippled man)

Today, many religious believers continue to believe that God performs miracles and that we should not be surprised to hear about miraculous events. Some take place in huge gatherings, others in a church or quietly as people pray for healing.

Some Christians believe that if God is all loving and all powerful then we shouldn't be surprised that he performs miracles. If he did so during biblical times, then there is no reason not to expect him to continue to do so today, since God is unchanging and eternal.

Benny Hinn is a Palestinian-Canadian evangelistic who conducts huge meetings where many people claim to have been miraculously healed

Believing in God

Arguments against miracles

- There is no need for God to perform miracles when we have the knowledge in the modern world to work things out ourselves
- Why would God heal some people and not others?
- People may not be truthful about experiencing miracles
- Why doesn't God perform miracles in situations that people would really notice?
- We cannot prove they have happened — there is always a good alternative explanation for the event

Religious Studies

Prayer

Prayer is perhaps the most common way in which religious believers communicate with God. It may involve words, or be silent (as in **meditation**), but in either case prayer assumes that God has a relationship with those who pray to him. Believers in God are likely to feel closer to God through prayer, especially when they take time to listen to God as well as speak to him. Prayer can take many forms:

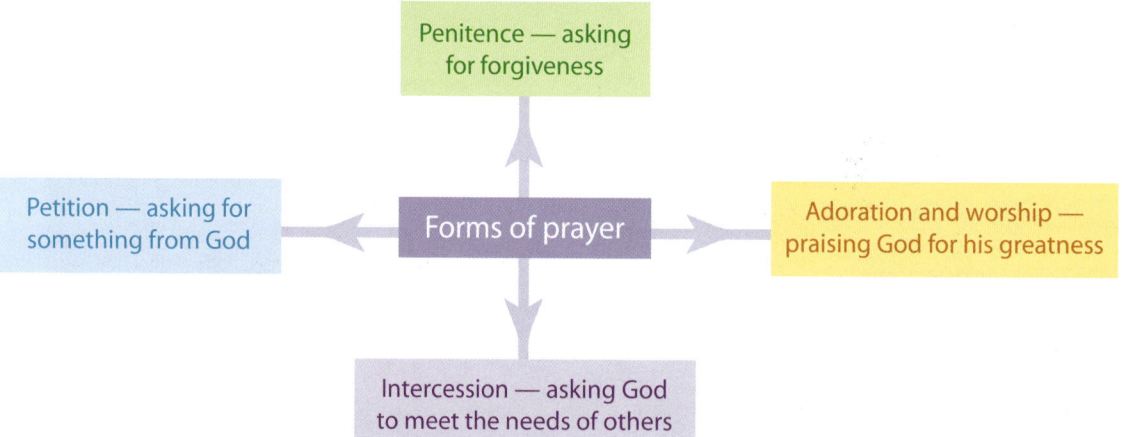

Prayers may be private and individual, or may be corporate — when a number of people pray the same prayer together. They may be formal, such as the Lord's Prayer, or spontaneous, when people make up a prayer to meet a particular need.

> Jesus taught: 'Ask and it will be given to you; search and you will find; knock, and the door will be opened for you. For everyone who asks receives, and everyone who searches finds, and for everyone who knocks, the door will be opened' (Matthew 7:7–8)

In most cases people pray because they already believe in God's existence but, on some occasions, people may come to believe in God because someone has told them about a prayer that was answered, or they may just try for themselves to see if a prayer might meet a need. If it does, or if in some way they believe that God has heard and answered the prayer, they may feel that they have good reasons to believe in God for themselves.

Key words

Confession of sins — admitting wrongdoing against God

Intercession — praying for others

Meditation — thinking deeply about spiritual things

Miracle — an event that only God could perform

Petitions — making requests of God

Thanksgiving — giving thanks to God for what he has done

Worship — praising God

Test yourself

1 What three characteristics should a miracle have?

2 Take the following biblical accounts of miracles and answer these questions about them:
   - Mark 5:35–41 (the calming of the storm)
   - Luke 8:40–56 (Jairus's daughter and the woman with the haemorrhage)
   - Matthew 14:13–21 (the feeding of the 5,000)
   - John 11:1–44 (the raising of Lazarus)
   - Acts 3–10 (the healing of the crippled man

   i Describe what happens in the event
   ii Why is it a miracle?
   iii Who benefits?
   iv How do people respond?
   v What do you think is the meaning of the event?

3 Do you think that we should believe someone who says that a miracle has happened? Explain the reasons for your answer.

4 What is prayer?

5 Explain **three** different types of prayer.

Examination question

a **What is meant by a miracle?** (2 marks)

b **Do you think that God still performs miracles? Give two reasons for your view.** (6 marks)

c **Why do some people reject the belief that God can perform miracles?** (8 marks)

d **'Praying to God makes no difference to anything.'**
   i **Do you agree? Give reasons for your view.** (3 marks)
   ii **Give reasons why some people may disagree with you.** (3 marks)

Exam tip

You should be able to recount accurately one biblical miracle and offer two or three clear points about its meaning and significance.

Topic 5
The arguments from causation and design

The existence of the world and its special features are often used by religious believers to support their belief in God. Their argument essentially runs thus:
- Nothing can come into existence on its own — everything needs a cause.
- The universe must therefore need a cause.
- Only God could be powerful enough to bring the universe into existence and to keep it going.
- Therefore God exists.

This is called an argument from **causation**, and it depends on our accepting as true the fact that everything is caused by something else and that the universe could not cause itself. This is a very old argument for the existence of God and in Christianity it is associated most often with Thomas Aquinas. He wrote:

In the cosmos as we experience it, it is obvious to us that some things change. Now, whatever changes must be changed by another. And if that other itself changes then that too must be changed by another. But this cannot go on to infinity…You eventually have to arrive at something that is unchanging. This is God.

Does this prove the existence of God?

Those who support the argument say it does, because:
- The only alternative is to accept that the world came about by chance.
- We explain everything else, so why not the world?
- The Bible teaches that God is the creator, so this argument backs it up.

However, some reject the view that it proves the existence of God, because:
- We don't know that everything is caused, we just make that assumption.
- Even if the universe is caused, it need not be caused by the Christian God.
- There are better explanations than God — the big bang theory, for example.
- We should just accept that the universe is here and not try to find a special reason for it.

It is not only the existence of the universe that leads some people to believe in God, or which confirms for them that an all powerful God must exist, but the features of the universe also. One feature is that of **design**. When we describe something as designed, we usually mean that it has a purpose of some kind — a function for which someone designed and made it. When we use something that has been designed, we are using something that has been designed and made by a person — we would not usually think of something being designed by nothing, or having been designed by luck or chance. That person has made choices about how to design whatever it is in the best possible way.

The argument from design runs in this way:
- Things that are designed are designed by someone who has used intelligence and thought.
- The universe appears to have been designed.
- Someone with intelligence and thought must have designed the universe.
- Only God could design something as complex as the universe.
- Therefore God exists.

This is a very popular reason that some people offer for believing in God because:
- It encourages us to look closely at the world and to think whether it is more or less likely that it has come about by chance rather than being created by a loving and intelligent God.
- Beautiful things in the universe and things that are not necessary for human beings to survive are said to need a special explanation, since why should they exist unless someone had specially created them? This being is thought by religious believers to be God.
- The world seems to be an ideal environment for human beings. Can this be explained by chance or is it more likely that a loving God designed it for them to enjoy?

One of the best known examples of this argument was put forward in 1802 by the Reverend William Paley. It compares the world to a watch and claims that, just as a watch must be designed, so must the universe, since it has so many complex and special features. This is called an **analogy** — a comparison that helps by looking at something we know in order to understand something we don't know, so we can reach a conclusion about whether it is more likely to have come about by chance or to have been created by an all powerful God.

> **Key words**
>
> **Analogy** — a way of comparing two similar things to highlight their similarities
>
> **Causation** — the principle that everything is caused by something else
>
> **Design** — the appearance of order and purpose

Test yourself

1. List all the facts in support of the design argument, then list all those against. Which are the more convincing and why?
2. If you were God, would you have designed the world differently? Explain your answer.
3. How do you think a supporter of the design argument would explain natural disasters?
4. Do you agree that nothing can cause itself? Can you think of examples of anything that causes itself?
5. Supporters of the argument from causation believe that God is the best explanation for the existence of the universe. Do you agree? Give reasons for your view, and explain why some people might disagree with it.
6. What alternative explanations for the cause of the universe can you think of? List them and then write an argument against them alongside.

Examination question

a What is meant by causation? (2 marks)

b Do you think that that the universe appears to be designed? Give two reasons for your view. (6 marks)

c For what reasons do some people reject the ideas of the design argument? (8 marks)

d 'It is a waste of time thinking about the cause of the universe. It's just here and that's all there is to it.'
   i Do you agree? Give reasons for your view. (3 marks)
   ii Give reasons why some people may disagree with you. (3 marks)

Exam tip
Learn the name of one scholar associated with each of these arguments and, when you write about them, make sure you don't get them mixed up.

Topic 6
Scientific explanations of the origin of the world

Scientific explanations of the universe include theories such as the **big bang**. This is the theory that the universe came about through an explosion of matter and energy some 15 billion years ago, but what existed before this event is completely unknown and a matter of pure speculation. An atheist may argue that religious believers who claim that God existed before the explosion and perhaps in some way brought it about are basing that claim on something that cannot be proved and so can have no real value.

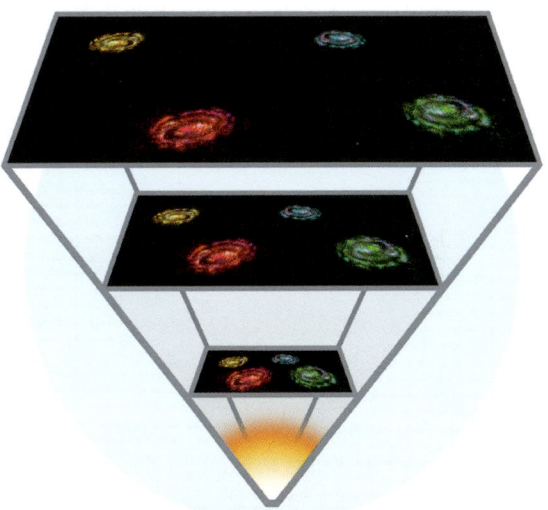

Another popular non-religious explanation is the theory of **natural selection**. This theory was popularised in the nineteenth century by Charles Darwin, who argued that all living things have descended from common ancestors and that each generation has adapted or evolved from more primitive forms of life, for example, modern species of dogs are descended from early wolves. The world itself is also in a process of **evolution** or change. Religious believers who reject this theory do so because it seems to do away with the need for God. Rather than living things being created fully formed, they gradually evolve from chemical matter, and need no personal, divine action.

Many nineteenth-century Christians were upset by Darwin's theory because it traced human origins back to apes, which seemed directly to contradict the creation story in Genesis 1–2.

Charles Darwin

Why are scientific explanations popular?

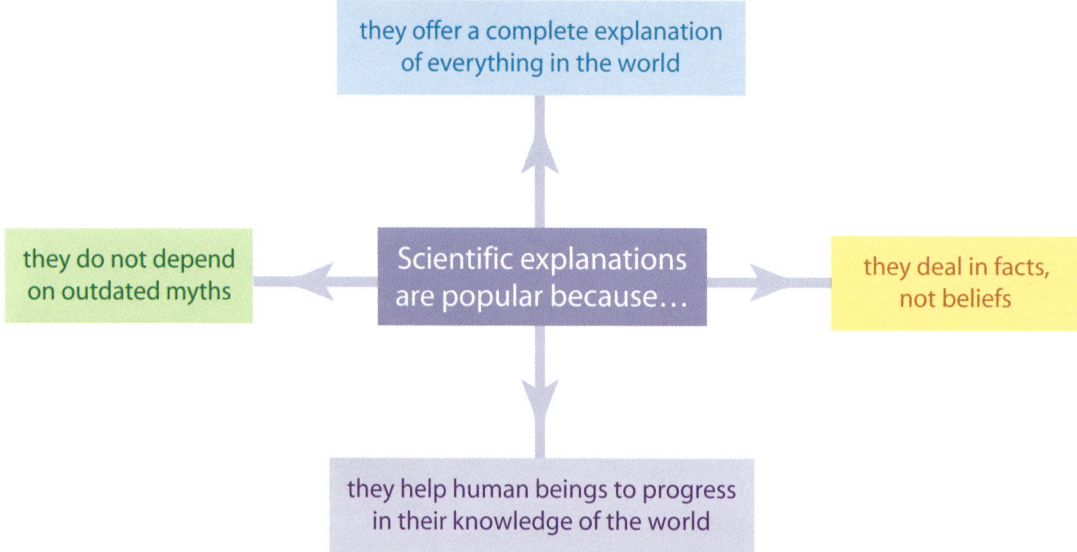

Richard Dawkins suggests that science does allow for some things to happen through a series of chances and he challenges the assumption made in the design argument that the universe has a purpose, arguing that it is humans who insist on finding purpose in everything because we look at the world through 'purpose coloured spectacles'.

Key words

Big bang theory — the theory that an enormous explosion started the universe around 15 billion years ago

Evolution — the gradual development of species over millions of years

Natural selection — the way in which species naturally select the best characteristics suited to survival

Test yourself

1. Richard Dawkins says that humans should not need to explain things by referring to God because we don't need more to marvel at than our own existence in the world. He says 'we are so grotesquely lucky to be here'. What do you think he means by this?

2. Do you think that science has proved that God does not exist? Think carefully about your answer to this question.

3. Why, do you think, were some Victorian Christians upset by Darwin's ideas about natural selection?

4. Find out more about (i) the big bang and (ii) evolution and natural selection and write short paragraphs about both.

Examination question

a What is the theory of natural selection? *(2 marks)*

b Do you think that science successfully explains the world without having to include God in that explanation? *(6 marks)*

c Why do some people support scientific views about the origin of the world? *(8 marks)*

d 'In the modern world, nobody should still believe that God created the world'.
  i Do you agree? Give reasons for your view. *(3 marks)*
  ii Give reasons why some people may disagree with you. *(3 marks)*

Exam tip

Don't make the assumption that all Christians reject scientific ideas about the existence of God. Many, if not most, accept them in some way today.

Topic 7
Christian responses to scientific explanations for the origins of the world

Some Christians believe that the only way to respond to scientific explanations of the world is to reject them as false. They argue that the accounts of creation in Genesis are the truth and can be supported by faith and evidence. Some Christians believe that the evidence of the world, including fossils, can prove that evolution is wrong and that the Genesis account reports creation as it happened. They also find verses in the Bible that support the evidence of the natural world, from which they believe physical laws of the universe have been derived.

- Creationist Christians believe that God created the world in 6 days in exactly the order and the manner described in Genesis.
- They are also sometimes called fundamentalists, which means that they accept all the teachings of the Bible as being true in every way.
- Some other Christians believe that the Genesis account is religiously true but not literally true. In other words, we learn about the process by which the world came into existence through scientific investigation, but we understand the relationship between God, humans and creation from the Bible.

An example of a Christian who is able to believe in God and who accepts scientific discoveries about the world is John Polkinghorne, a leading Christian writer and a scientist. He argues that both science and religion can be understood by reference to God and that physical explanations do not completely explain the universe. He says: 'Something of lasting significance is glimpsed in the beauty of the natural world.' (*Science and Christian Belief*, SPCK, 1994)

The **aesthetic argument**, which is adopted by some Christians, is based on the view that the world is so beautiful that it must be the work of God, who is a loving and powerful creator. Many Christian hymns and songs focus on this view:

All things bright and beautiful,
all creatures great and small,
all things wise and wonderful,
the Lord God made them all.

In recent times, some Christians have adopted the theory of **intelligent design**. The principle of intelligent design is that the biological structures of the world are so complex that they need intelligent causes to explain them and that we can find evidence for these causes. The theory claims that the idea of evolution happening without a designing intelligence behind it does not fit the evidence. Intelligent design is presented as a scientific approach, which is why it is unpopular with non-religious scientists who argue that it is really just a religious view.

> **Key words**
>
> **Aesthetic argument** — the argument for the existence of God based on the claim that the world is too beautiful to have come about by impersonal chance
>
> **Intelligent design** — the theory that the complexity of biological structures suggests that they must be designed by an intelligent mind

Test yourself

1 Read Genesis 1–2 and then explain how a creationist/fundamentalist Christian would explain the details, and then compare that response with a Christian who believes that the Bible is religiously, but not literally, true.

2 Do you think that the beauty of the world needs a special explanation? Can you think of a non-religious explanation for beauty?

3 Look at the picture of the creationist car (on page 24). What impression does this give of the views some Christians hold?

4 Use the internet to find out about intelligent design and write a paragraph explaining its principles. Make two criticisms of it and identify two possible strengths.

Examination question

a What is intelligent design? (2 marks)

b Do you think that Christians respond to non-religious explanations of the origin of the universe in a good way? Give two reasons for your view. (6 marks)

c Why do some Christians propose the aesthetic argument? (8 marks)

d 'The world is ugly, hard and unforgiving, not beautiful and orderly. God cannot have made it.'
  i Do you agree? Give reasons for your view. (3 marks)
  ii Give reasons why some people may disagree with you. (3 marks)

> **Exam tip**
>
> This is quite a difficult topic, because you must separate it from the design and cosmological arguments. Christians may come back to these to reinforce their views, but they were not originally intended to be responses to scientific explanations.

Topic 8
Unanswered prayer

- Prayers that appear to go unanswered by God can lead people away from belief in him. An atheist may claim that, if a loving God exists, then unanswered prayers are a real problem, since surely he should answer the prayers of all those who pray in faith and who truly believe.
- It may even be possible to claim that a truly good God would answer the prayers of anyone who prayed, not just those who believe in him.
- Unanswered prayers test the faith of believers too, and it seems natural for anyone who has prayed sincerely to ask 'Why not?' when God appears to have said 'no' to their requests.
- Many people experience suffering and pain in their own lives and the lives of their family and friends and, when God seems to do nothing about it, it may be easy to reject belief in him.
- For some atheists, the suffering in the world persuades them that there is no God, especially when people praying all over the world seem to make no difference.

Christians also struggle with the problem of unanswered prayer, which can be a big challenge to their faith. Some may turn away from God.

Christians have to accept that, although God hears and answers prayer, he does not always answer in the way that they hope he will. Sometimes God's answer to a request is 'no' and they have to try to understand God's answer and grow closer in their relationship with him.

Others, however, believe that, if their prayer seems to be unanswered, it is because what they are praying for is not part of God's will or God's plan. God is not there just to grant whatever prayers a Christian asks but those that help him or her to fulfil God's plans for the world. Humans cannot always understand this, but God knows best.

Test yourself

1 Give examples of **three** types of prayer that God could not, or would not, answer. Explain your answers.

2 How do you think religious believers would explain it if God did not answer their prayers as they hoped in these circumstances:
   – to heal their mum of cancer
   – to pass their exams
   – to become a pop star
   – to stop being bullied
   – to show them a miracle

3 Do you think God should care about the prayers of individuals or only those prayers that affect everyone — such as praying for peace in the world?

Examination question

a **What is prayer?** *(2 marks)*

b **Do you think God should answer every prayer that is for something good and true? Give two reasons for your answer.** *(6 marks)*

c **Why do you think God does not answer all prayers in the way that people hope he will?** *(8 marks)*

d **'Prayer is a waste of time; we should solve our own problems.'**
  i **Do you agree? Give reasons for your view.** *(3 marks)*
  ii **Give reasons why some people may disagree with you.** *(3 marks)*

Exam tip
Remember that for God to answer a prayer he doesn't have to say 'yes'. The whole issue here is about accepting that God's answer to a prayer is sometimes 'no'.

Topic 9
The problem of evil and suffering

One of the strongest reasons given for atheism is the problem of evil. This ties up closely with what religious believers claim to be true about the nature of God. The problem can be expressed in this way:

- God is thought to be all loving and all good (omni-benevolent), all powerful (omnipotent) and all knowing (omniscient).
- If God is omni-benevolent he would want to remove evil and suffering.
- If God is omniscient he would know how to remove evil and suffering.
- If God is omnipotent he would be able to remove evil and suffering.
- Therefore, both God and evil cannot exist.
- It is not reasonable to deny the existence of evil and suffering, since they are experienced in some way by most people.
- **Therefore God cannot exist**.

This is a very powerful argument as it challenges the existence and the attributes (characteristics) of God. If God exists but is not perfect then he isn't actually the God in whom religious people believe. If he isn't all good and loving, why should people devote their lives to serving him? Because these problems are so serious, religious believers have either to abandon their belief in God or find a convincing explanation for why God allows evil to continue and yet is still all loving and all powerful.

This can be illustrated in the form of the inconsistent triad.

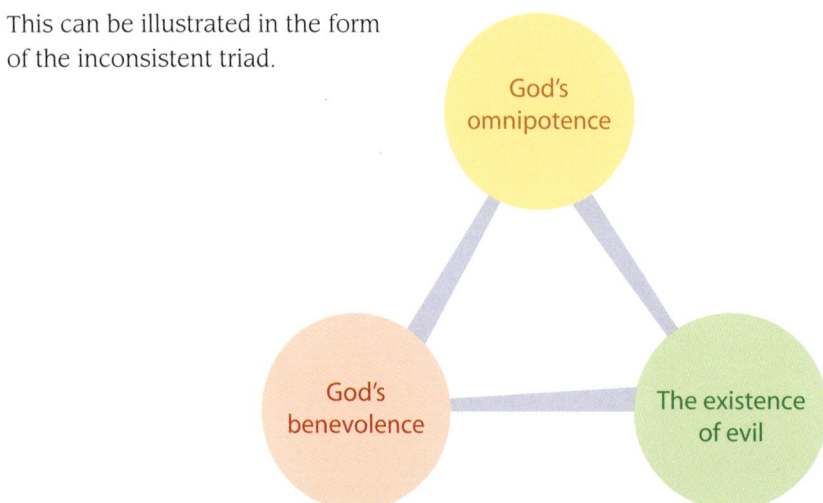

The religious believer cannot deny that any of these three elements is true — they are committed to believing that God is all powerful and all loving, and it would be foolish to suggest that evil does not exist. However, together, all three elements present a problem that needs to be resolved.

Traditionally, there are thought to be two types of evil:
- **moral evil** — evil actions performed by human beings, and the evil consequences of such actions — e.g. murder, rape, war, theft

The 9/11 attacks on New York, where two hijacked planes crashed and destroyed the World Trade Center

- **natural evil** — faults and flaws in the natural world that are beyond human control, e.g. famine, disease, natural disasters and freak weather conditions

The aftermath of the 2004 tsunami in southeast Asia

These two types of evil can overlap, for instance, the evil of war can lead to the natural evil of famine. Human greed often limits natural resources to the wealthiest in society.

If the existence of evil and suffering counts against God's love and power, then does he exist at all? Some believers may suggest that perhaps evil and suffering don't exist and are just in human imagination. Others may suggest that God does not need to be both all loving and all powerful. However, for most believers these are not satisfactory solutions and they need to find a way to solve the problem without denying the existence of God or the existence of suffering.

Christian responses to the problem of evil

Christians have traditionally thought it very important to respond to the problem of evil. One of the oldest responses is based on the accounts of creation and the Fall in Genesis 1–3.

The Genesis accounts suggest that God created the world and human beings perfectly and that he gave humans free will — this is the ability to be able to make choices without being influenced by outside forces. For example, a telephone cannot make free choices, neither can any other non-living object. On the other hand, human beings are able to make a vast range of choices, some of which are not very significant, but some have an effect on other people and we have to make them wisely. We can choose to do things that cause harm or good and, when these choices are made freely, they have real meaning. If we are made to do things because we are told they are good, but we don't do them freely, we are less likely to learn positive things from them, or become more morally developed human beings.

- The Genesis story teaches that the first human beings, Adam and Eve, chose to use their free will to disobey the command God gave them not to eat of the fruit of the tree of the knowledge of good and evil.
- When they did eat it, sin and suffering were brought into the world by their freely chosen actions and, as a result, God dealt out certain punishments: pain in childbirth, male domination, poor harvests and, most importantly, separation from God.
- Christians who accept this account also believe that God had already planned the coming of Jesus to die and rise to bring sinful humanity back into a relationship with God, so the outcome was not all negative.

A similar way of responding to the problem of evil claims that, if we make genuine choices to do good, we can help humanity become better and contribute to the world becoming a better place. Many Christians believe that the choices we make also have an influence on where will go after death — they can grow closer to God or further away from him, and the existence of suffering helps people to make choices that please God: comforting the bereaved, feeding the hungry, and preserving the environment, for example. Furthermore, unless we know what it means to suffer, the bliss of heaven will not have the same meaning for us.

Ultimately, however, many Christians claim that we cannot ever really understand God's reasons for allowing evil and suffering to continue in a world that he controls, but this should not cause us to doubt his love because, even if his reasons are not clear to human beings, he works with a final plan in view, which is all good and all loving.

> **Key words**
>
> **Moral evil** — actions performed by human beings that cause suffering to humans and animals
>
> **Natural evil** — events in the natural order of things that cause suffering to humans and animals

Test yourself

1 Using examples, explain the difference between natural and moral evil.
2 Look at today's newspaper and make a list of all the news stories involving suffering. Identify those that are about moral evil and those that are about natural evil. Some may be a mixture of both. Say what caused each incident and how it might have been prevented.
3 Does evil always lead to suffering? Is suffering always wrong?
4 How do you think God would respond to human questions about evil and suffering?
5 Explain **two** Christian responses to the problem of evil and suffering.
6 Do you think these are good solutions? Devise a solution that you think is better.

Examination question

a What is moral evil? *(2 marks)*

b Do you think that evil and suffering should lead Christians to question their belief in God? Give two reasons for your answer. *(6 marks)*

c Why do some people believe that suffering should not count against belief in God? *(8 marks)*

d Suffering is necessary to become close to God
   i Do you agree? Give reasons for your view. *(3 marks)*
   ii Give reasons why some people may disagree with you. *(3 marks)*

Exam tip
A traditional Christian solution to the problem of evil and suffering is known as a theodicy.

Topic 10
Religious programming on television and radio

Religious programmes on television take various forms.
- Some are directed at religious believers, offering them worship and teaching, such as *Songs of Praise*.
- Some are also of interest to non-believers because they address religious issues and encourage debate and discussion of different views.
- When religious broadcasting first began in the UK it was directed at Christians, but now it reflects a range of religious beliefs.
- Today, people are very interested in religion even if they are not religious and want to find out about different religious views, especially about difficult issues. Television programmes respond to this interest.

A programme such as *Songs of Praise* is more likely to confirm how people feel about religion since it is directed at people who already believe in God. It is a regular programme, shown on Sunday evenings on BBC1. It has a magazine format, meaning that it features interviews, musical items, readings and clips from religious services, often focusing on a particular church or local community. The programme features individuals who have faced and overcome difficulties, or people whose religious belief has led them to make a significant contribution to society, and who may be an inspiration to viewers.

The programme aims to be contemporary and relevant as well as reflecting traditional aspects of the Christian faith, so the music featured is very varied. This helps the programme to appeal to a range of religious believers and for those who are new to religious programmes to hear music they might usually associate with rock or pop concerts, and be drawn in to listening.

The BBC radio stations offer a wide range of religious programmes. If you look at the website www.bbc.co.uk/radio/programmes/genres/religionandethics/player you will see that many aspects of religious belief and interest are featured, from Hindu devotional music, to debates about moral issues, to traditional Christian worship services, and so they reflect the range of religious beliefs in the country. They also need to reflect the interest in religious matters shared by many non-religious people.

Radio 2 presents a weekly programme every Sunday from 7–9 a.m. called *Good Morning Sunday*, with Aled Jones. The programme features music from a variety of styles, including traditional Christian choral music, modern Christian music and spiritual music that encourages meditation and restfulness. The programme also features interviews on religious and ethical issues as well as general interest articles and interviews.

Religious Studies

The BBC also broadcasts the *Daily Service* and a weekly *Choral Evensong*. The key feature of this broadcast is choral music, so it appeals to those who enjoy the choral music tradition.

There are many other religious programmes on the radio, several of which address issues of ethics and morality. These include the popular programme *The Moral Maze,* which addresses issues of general ethical interest as well as those of particular concern to religious believers.

On the BBC webpage **www.bbc.co.uk/religion/programmes/** you will find that most specifically religious programmes, however, are devotional. This means that they help people to think deeply about their faith and to consider issues that would not usually be of interest to the general listener.

Test yourself

1. Does religious radio broadcasting offer anything for young people or is it only for older people?
2. List the ways in which religious programmes may help the faith of religious believers.
3. Give reasons why such programmes may turn people off religion.
4. 'Religious programmes should be banned.' Do you agree? Give reasons for your view.
5. If you were to devise a religious television or radio show, what would you include in it and who would be your guests?
6. Describe **one** religious programme on television and **one** on radio. Explain how this particular programme may help the faith of a believer OR help someone come to believe in God.

Matters of life and death

Topic 11
Christian and Islamic beliefs about life after death

The question of whether or not there is life after death is one of the greatest mysteries. There are many different viewpoints held by both religious believers and non-believers. The question revolves around what, if anything, survives death and is what survives really us?

Why do people believe in life after death?

All physical life ends, yet, for many people, not just religious believers, this is hard to accept, and the prospect of life after death is very desirable.

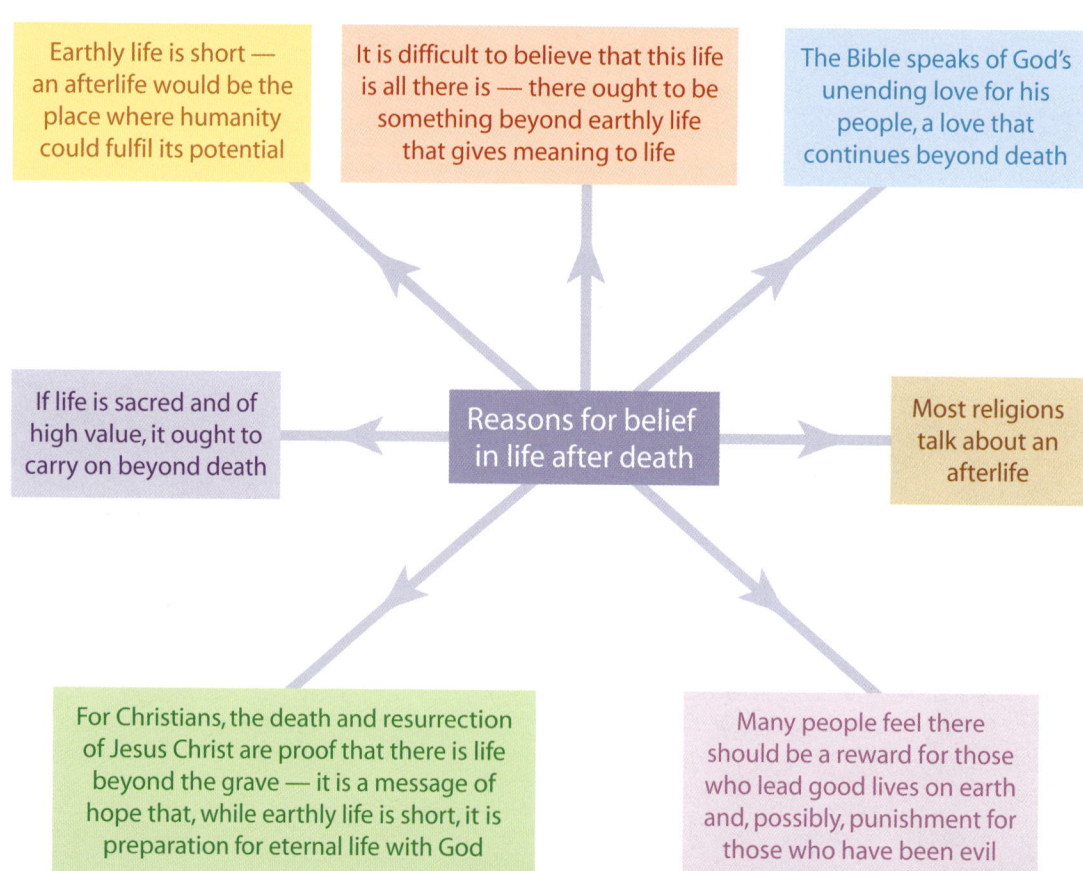

- Earthly life is short — an afterlife would be the place where humanity could fulfil its potential
- It is difficult to believe that this life is all there is — there ought to be something beyond earthly life that gives meaning to life
- The Bible speaks of God's unending love for his people, a love that continues beyond death
- If life is sacred and of high value, it ought to carry on beyond death
- **Reasons for belief in life after death**
- Most religions talk about an afterlife
- For Christians, the death and resurrection of Jesus Christ are proof that there is life beyond the grave — it is a message of hope that, while earthly life is short, it is preparation for eternal life with God
- Many people feel there should be a reward for those who lead good lives on earth and, possibly, punishment for those who have been evil

Christian belief in the afterlife

Christians usually adopt one of two approaches to understanding the afterlife:

Immortality of the soul

This is the belief that humans have a physical body and a spiritual, **immortal soul**, which is their real self. The soul survives the death of the physical body and goes to exist in a spiritual realm, such as heaven. This idea is known as dualism since it rests on the belief that there are two parts to human nature — the physical and the spiritual.

Such a viewpoint however, does have problems:
- Is the immortal soul really a person? One might argue that a person without a body is not a person at all.
- Where do souls actually go when the body dies? Thomas Aquinas suggested three possible places:
  - hell — a place of eternal punishment for the worst people
  - purgatory — a place where Christians who have lapsed in their faith may undergo a period of punishment and purification
  - beatific vision/heaven — a place of everlasting joy and happiness, where God dwells. This is the eternal home for faithful Christians and those who have completed purgatory.

However, many people, including a number of Christians, do not believe in hell, saying that an all powerful, loving God could not allow such a place to exist. Moreover, they claim, eternal life should be available to all humanity, and not just Christians.

Many people do not believe in hell, saying that a loving God would not allow such a place to exist

Bodily resurrection

The doctrine of **bodily resurrection** suggests that, by an act of God's love, the dead will one day be restored to life again in bodily form. At a future date, there will be the Day of Judgement, when the dead will be raised and God will judge the world. Evil will be banished forever and the righteous will be rewarded with eternal life:

> 'He will repay according to each one's deeds: to those who by patiently doing good seek for glory and honour and immortality, he will give eternal life.' (Romans 2:6–7)

> 'I saw the dead, great and small, standing before the throne…Another book was opened, the book of life. And the dead were judged according to their works…and anyone whose name was not found written in the book of life was thrown into the lake of fire.' (Revelation 20:12,15)

The resurrection of Jesus Christ himself, who appears to the disciples after his death, is the model for this view of the afterlife. Jesus talks to them, eats with them and they can touch him. *'Look at my hands and my feet. It is I myself! Touch me and see, a ghost does not have flesh and bones, as you see I have'* (Luke 24:39). Later in the New Testament, Paul explains that the resurrected body, even though it looks the same as the physical body, is spiritual and therefore cannot die: *'So will it be with the resurrection of the dead. The body that is sown is perishable, it is raised imperishable…it is sown in a natural body, it is raised a spiritual body'* (1 Corinthians 15:42–44).

There are difficulties with the doctrine of bodily resurrection:
- If a person is resurrected is it still really the same person or something that just looks like the person?
- If God re-creates individuals, what do they look like — do they look as they were at the moment they died or at some other point in their lives?
- What about people who have disabilities on earth — will they still have these disabilities in eternal life?
- Where do all these bodies live? Isn't there a problem with overcrowding?

Islamic belief in the afterlife

Belief in **Akhira**, or life after death, is very important for Muslims. Islam teaches that the soul will be judged and will thereafter be sent to paradise or hell. On the Day of Judgement God will raise everyone from the dead and recreate their bodies to an exact replica of the body they had on earth. Heaven will be a beautiful place of great joy, but hell will be a place of sorrow and torment. To avoid hell, a Muslim must be a faithful follower of the Qur'an and the Shariah law and, although most Muslims believe that all non-Muslims will go to hell, some suggest that non-Muslims who have led good lives will also go to heaven.

Key words

Akhira — life after death

Immortality of the soul — the belief that humans have a body that will die, and a soul or spirit that can live on after the death of the body

Janannam — hell

Jannat — heaven

Resurrection of the body — the belief that God will raise the physical body to life again after death

Muslim beliefs about the afterlife

- Individuals can never be sure that they know how God will judge them in the afterlife: 'The unbelievers say, "Never to us will come the hour"…But most surely, he may reward those who believe and work deeds of righteousness, for such is forgiveness and a sustenance most generous' (Surah 34:3–5)

- Two angels open the book containing the record of what the person has done when alive on earth: names on the right-hand side of the book will be sent to paradise, but those recorded on the left-hand side will be sent to hell

- As a result of judgement, the soul will be sent to paradise (**Jannat**) or to hell (**Janannam**)

- The angel of death will first take a person's soul to barzakh – the stage between the moment of death and the moment of facing judgement

- Everyone will try to reach paradise over the Assirat Bridge: those whose destiny is to go to hell will fall off in the attempt

- Earthly life is observed by Allah, and everything Muslims do and say is recorded and assessed for the afterlife

- Islamic belief in the resurrection means that Muslims are not cremated, but are buried so that their body is ready to be raised by God

- Surah 56:115–21 teaches that those who live a good life will '… sit on gold-encrusted thrones of happiness…Immortal youths will wait upon them with…cups filled with water from pure springs…and with fruit of any kind that they choose'

- Whether a person will spend eternity in heaven or hell is entirely up to Allah: 'Their status in Heaven and Hell may last for eternity, but this is subject to God's will and mercy' (Surah 11:106–108)

As with some Christians, not all Muslims believe that these ideas are literally true, but rather understand them as metaphors.

Test yourself

1. Explain **three** reasons why people might believe in an afterlife.
2. Which of these positions seems most convincing to you?
3. Read at least **two** Gospel accounts of the resurrection of Jesus. What are their key features? Do these accounts help us to believe in the possibility of an afterlife?
4. Are there good reasons to believe that we have a soul? Explain your answer in as much detail as possible.
5. What do you think Christians mean by saying that the fact that Jesus rose from the dead means that they can have an afterlife?
6. Find out what at least one Christian church teaches about the afterlife. You could start by looking up the Catechism of the Roman Catholic Church.
7. Explain the differences between Christian and Muslim understandings of life after death. If you find it hard to find any differences, think why this may be the case, then examine the teachings of the two religions again.
8. 'The idea of heaven is only for religious people.' Do you agree? Give reasons for your answers.

Examination question

a **What is meant by the resurrection of the body?** *(2 marks)*

b **Do you agree that Christian belief must include belief in the afterlife? Give two reasons for your view.** *(6 marks)*

c **Why do some Christians or Muslims accept the idea of heaven and hell and others do not?** *(8 marks)*

d **'The idea of the afterlife is just for people who can't cope with the prospect of death.'**
   i **Do you agree? Give reasons for your view.** *(3 marks)*
   ii **Give reasons why some people may disagree with you.** *(3 marks)*

Exam tip

Christians and Muslims base their beliefs in the afterlife on what the Bible/Qur'an and the Church (for Christians) teach, not on what psychics or mediums claim to prove, so never mention ghosts or even near-death experiences as a reason for Christians or Muslims to believe in life after death.

Topic 12
Non-religious belief in life after death

People have different views on what happens when we die. For those who are not religious believers, there are several possibilities:
- Nothing happens because this life is all there is and when we die we die.
- We become ghosts.
- We join the spiritual world.
- We are reincarnated into another physical life, either human or animal. This view is a very important part of the belief system of some Eastern religions. However, many non-religious believers also argue that this is the most satisfactory way for them to understand an afterlife.

In the modern world, therefore, there are many non-religious views concerning life after death. This might be for some of the same reasons that Christians and Muslims have for believing that life must continue beyond the grave, but without the key idea that it is associated with belief in God, the resurrection of Jesus, or expectation of judgment at the end of time.

Non-religious reasons for belief in the afterlife

Two of the most widespread non-religious reasons to believe in the afterlife are **near-death experiences** and the **paranormal**.

Near-death experiences

Scientists have, in recent years, examined the cases of many people who have died (perhaps during a surgical operation) and later been resuscitated. In a near-death experience the people who had died described a feeling of floating out of their bodies and then travelling down a tunnel to emerge into another world. Here they met Jesus, or a figure associated with their own religious tradition. Non-religious believers claimed to meet a dead relative or friend. Between them and the figure was often a barrier or gate. At this point, they are forced to make a choice whether to cross the barrier, or to return to earth. Obviously, the people describing these experiences opted to return to earthly life.

But are such accounts really proof of life after death? It has been argued that such accounts may be hallucinations caused by a lack of oxygen to the brain. Alternatively, they could be dreams, or lost subconscious memories. In other words, near-death experiences may be interesting phenomena but they do not, of themselves, prove the existence of life after death. However, it is not likely that a religious believer would accept NDE or paranormal experiences as sufficient proof of an afterlife in themselves.

Religious Studies

The paranormal (parapsychology)

Groups such as the Spiritualist Movement have claimed that there is a spirit world beyond this one, where people's spirits live on after death and which can be reached through séances and mediums. A problem with this is that the Spiritualist Movement has, over the years, been the subject of much ridicule, and many hoaxers have made it appear bogus. Moreover, what is the point of the spirit world? Is it just to continue life as it is on earth, or is there something more?

An account in 1 Samuel 28 tells how the witch or medium of Endor communicated with the spirit of the dead prophet Samuel even though the Law of Moses in the Old Testament expressly forbids people to become mediums: 'A man or woman who is a medium or spiritualist among you must be put to death' (Leviticus 20:27).

Non-belief in the afterlife

Many non-religious people do not believe in any form of the afterlife.

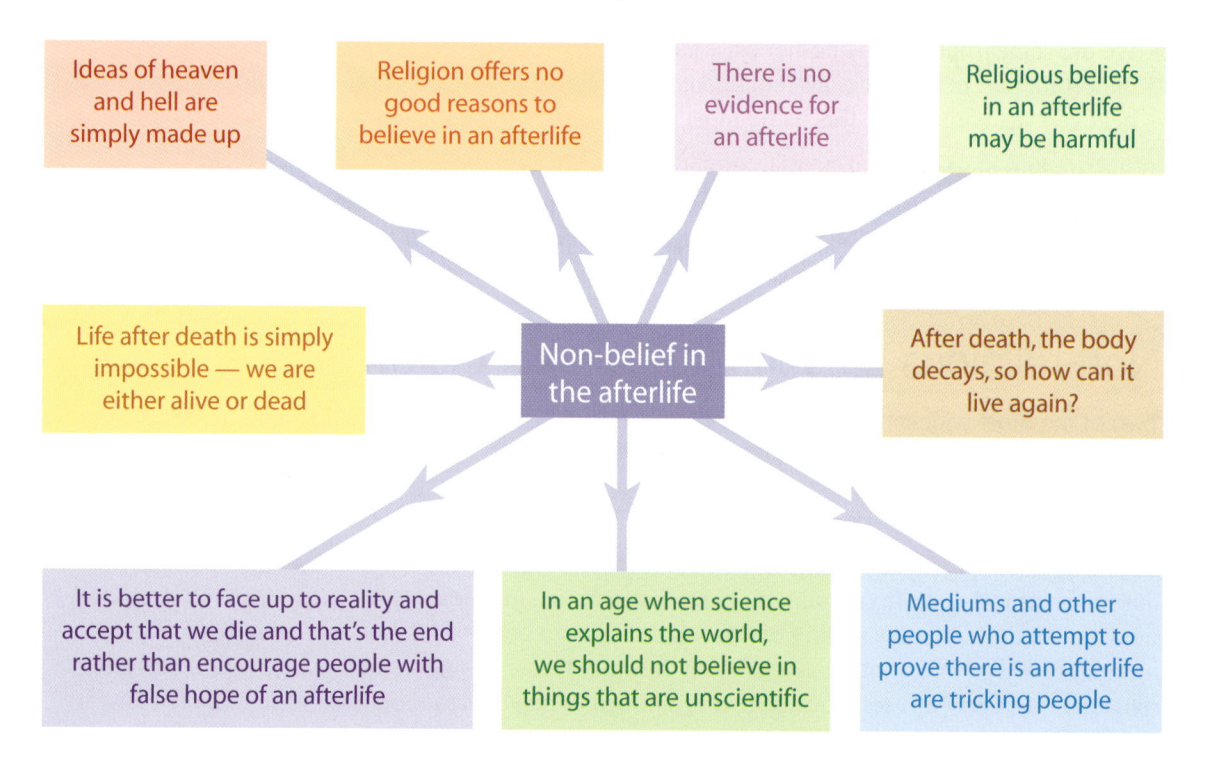

- Ideas of heaven and hell are simply made up
- Religion offers no good reasons to believe in an afterlife
- There is no evidence for an afterlife
- Religious beliefs in an afterlife may be harmful
- Life after death is simply impossible — we are either alive or dead
- **Non-belief in the afterlife**
- After death, the body decays, so how can it live again?
- It is better to face up to reality and accept that we die and that's the end rather than encourage people with false hope of an afterlife
- In an age when science explains the world, we should not believe in things that are unscientific
- Mediums and other people who attempt to prove there is an afterlife are tricking people

Some of these ideas are based on quite sophisticated philosophical problems, such as the question of whether we have any personal identity after we have died. If so, then what is it that survives — the soul or the body? If both ideas seem unconvincing, then we cannot talk of an afterlife.

Some atheists, such as Richard Dawkins, have genuine concerns about the way in which teaching about heaven and hell can alarm or control believers. Some churches, particularly in the USA, put on productions called Hell House Outreaches, plays that show non-believers going to hell because they have done supposedly terrible things. The plays show people suffering pain, torment and terrible unhappiness in hell, and it is suggested that this may distress people who see them. Christians who put on these productions might argue that it is better to be frightened now than risk going to hell.

> **Key words**
>
> **Near-death experience** — an unusual experience occurring when someone is on the verge of death, and recalled afterwards; often a vision of light, a tunnel or out-of-body experience
>
> **Paranormal** — events or experiences presumed to be beyond normal scientific understanding

Test yourself

1 List all the reasons you think may support life after death and those that count against it. Decide which view you think is more convincing and explain your answer.

2 Is it a satisfactory view to say that this life is all there is and there is no good reason to hope for the afterlife? Explain your answer.

3 Could science ever prove or disprove the claim that there is life after death? Give reasons for and against both views.

4 Do you think that life after death is an exciting prospect? Explain your answer.

5 Do you think that it is possible to believe in the afterlife without believing in God?

6 If it were possible to prove the existence of ghosts, would this prove the existence of an afterlife?

7 Do you agree that belief in the afterlife is only for those who aren't prepared to face up to the truths of human existence? If so, how would you try to persuade them that they are wrong?

Examination question

a **What is a near-death experience?** *(2 marks)*

b **Do you agree that there are no good reasons to believe in an afterlife? Give two reasons for your view.** *(6 marks)*

c **Why do some non-religious believers accept the possibility of an afterlife?** *(8 marks)*

d **'The evidence of parapsychology for an afterlife is very strong.'**
   i **Do you agree? Give reasons for your view.** *(3 marks)*
   ii **Give reasons why some people may disagree with you.** *(3 marks)*

Exam tip

This is quite a sophisticated topic as it deals with philosophical questions about what is reasonable to believe based on our regular experience of the world. It could be a chance for you to shine with your understanding of these views.

Topic 13
Abortion

Abortion is the termination of the life of a foetus in the womb. A spontaneous or natural abortion is called a miscarriage. When carried out by doctors, this is called a surgical or therapeutic abortion. It is abortion in this sense that we shall deal with.

Abortion presents serious problems for both religious and non-religious people. The main argument concerns the question of whether or not the foetus in the womb is a human being. There are two conflicting viewpoints:

1 'It is wrong to take human life. A foetus is human life, therefore abortion is wrong.'
2 'It is wrong to take human life. However, a foetus is not a human life, therefore abortion is not wrong.'

When does human life begin?
- At the moment of fertilisation?
- At the moment when the fertilised egg is implanted into the wall of the womb?
- At the moment when the foetus moves within the womb (the quickening)?
- At the point when the foetus could, in principle, be capable of being born alive and exist independent of the mother?
- At birth?

Until 1967, abortions were illegal in the UK. This meant that women who wanted abortions had to resort to what were known as back-street abortions, often performed by unqualified people, and which on many occasions resulted in infection and sometimes the death of the woman. Supporters of legalised abortion claimed that women who want abortions will try to get them by any means, legal or not and that legalising abortions would save such women from further suffering.

As a result, abortions were legalised by the Abortion Act 1967 (amended 1990), which allows abortion, but only if two doctors agree on the following conditions:
- The mother's life is at risk.
- The mother's physical or mental health is at risk.
- The child might be born seriously handicapped.
- There is a risk to the health of other existing children.

An abortion must be carried out up to the 24th week of pregnancy: after this time the child in the womb is considered to be capable of survival outside the womb. Later abortions are therefore permitted only if the mother's life is at risk.

Arguments in support of abortion

1 The woman's right to choose
Those who support the practice of abortion usually justify it on the grounds of the rights of the mother to make choices.

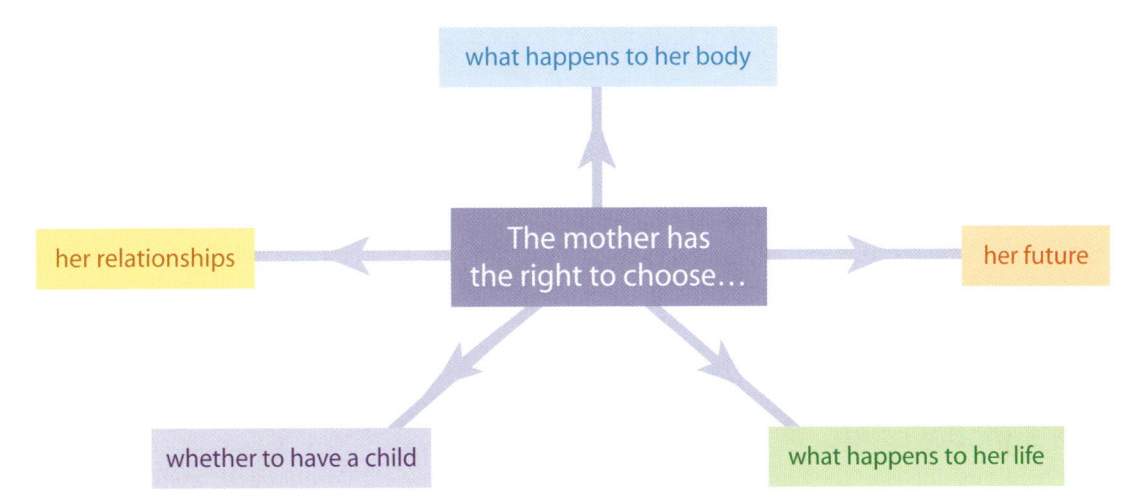

The mother has the right to choose…
- what happens to her body
- her relationships
- her future
- whether to have a child
- what happens to her life

2 The quality of life
The quality of life that the unborn child can expect is also an important consideration. It may be argued that the foetus has the right to a life free from pain and to be a wanted child. If these things are not possible, then abortion may be the best option.

3 The doctrine of double effect
This is the principle that, while an abortion is undesirable, it may be carried out if the primary purpose is not to destroy the foetus but to save the mother's life. The loss of the foetus is the secondary outcome of the abortion, not the primary purpose of carrying it out.

4 Population growth
Some politicians have argued that abortion helps to keep population numbers down. This may be particularly the case in traditionally Roman Catholic countries such as Brazil, which suffer from poverty and overcrowding. However, many would see this as a very harsh way to limit population, and encourage better teaching on contraception to avoid this.

Arguments against abortion

Anti-abortionist groups, such as LIFE and The Society for the Protection of the Unborn Child, argue that the foetus is a human being and therefore has rights:

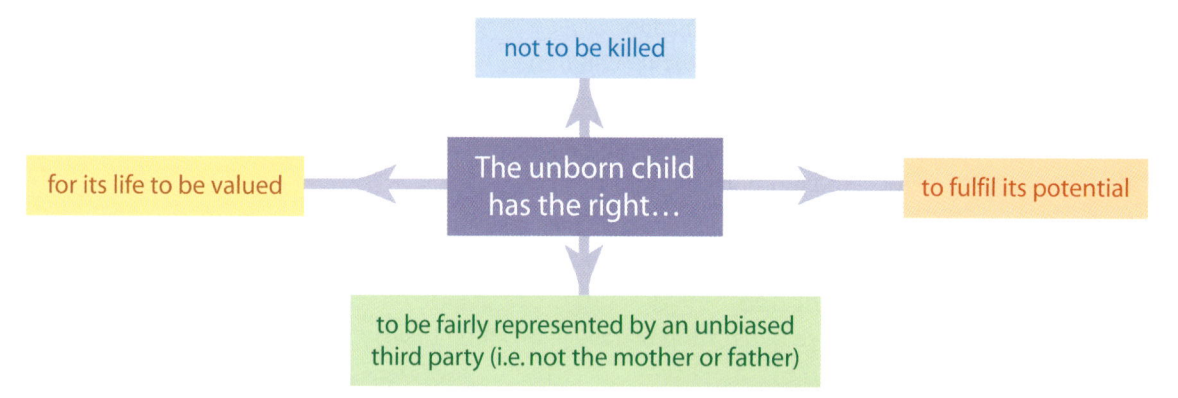

The unborn child has the right…
- not to be killed
- for its life to be valued
- to fulfil its potential
- to be fairly represented by an unbiased third party (i.e. not the mother or father)

In such cases, the rights of the foetus take precedence over those of the mother and aborting a foetus is considered to be no different from killing any other human being. It is wrong to kill a foetus just because it is handicapped, because having a baby might affect the mother's life or career, or to suggest that certain unborn babies would be better off remaining unborn.

> **Exam tip**
> Don't use the phrase 'pro-abortionists'. Those who support the woman's right to have an abortion do so because they support her right to make choices about her life and her body, not because they think that abortion is, in itself, a good thing.

Christian attitudes to abortion

The sanctity of life

For Christians, life is of the highest value and, although they have different views about abortion, they will be influenced in some way by belief in the principle of **the sanctity of life**.

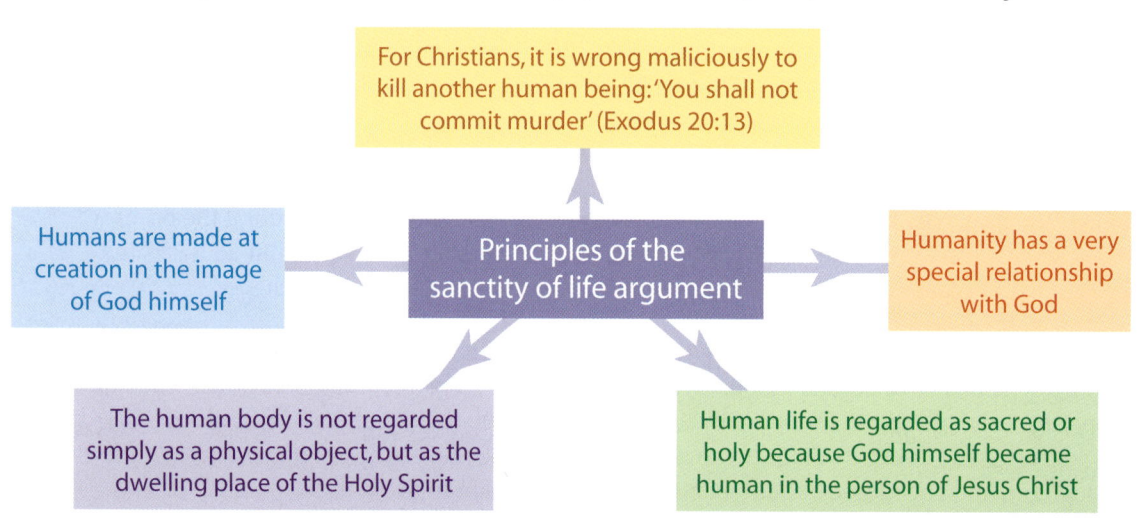

Principles of the sanctity of life argument
- For Christians, it is wrong maliciously to kill another human being: 'You shall not commit murder' (Exodus 20:13)
- Humans are made at creation in the image of God himself
- Humanity has a very special relationship with God
- The human body is not regarded simply as a physical object, but as the dwelling place of the Holy Spirit
- Human life is regarded as sacred or holy because God himself became human in the person of Jesus Christ

'So God created humankind in his image, in the image of God he created them; male and female he created them' (Genesis 1:27).

'If we live, we live to the Lord: if we die, we die to the Lord. So whether we live or die, we belong to the Lord' (Romans 14:8).

'Your body is a temple of the Holy Spirit, who is in you, whom you have received from God. You are not on your own…therefore honour God with your body' (1 Corinthians 6:19–20).

'God alone is the Lord of life…no one can under any circumstances claim for himself the right directly to destroy an innocent human being' (*Catechism of the Catholic Church*).

People view the birth of a baby as very special and usually want to protect and nurture it

How does this apply to abortion?

Many Christians — particularly Roman Catholics and conservative Evangelicals — are opposed to abortion on the following grounds:
- The sanctity of life — life is a sacred gift from God and only he can end a pregnancy.
- The Bible forbids the murder of human beings.
- Life begins at the moment of conception.
- The unborn child is created in the image of God.
- Every human being has the right to life.

Abortion is a horrible crime…the law must provide appropriate sanctions for every deliberate violation of the child's rights. (*Catechism of the Catholic Church*)

The Church of England and the Methodist Church agree that abortion is undesirable but, at the same time, it may be the lesser of two evils and, under some circumstances, the most loving thing to do. For instance, an abortion might be permissible in the case of rape, severe handicap or where the life of the mother is at risk.

We also believe that to withdraw compassion in circumstances of extreme distress or need is a very great evil. In an imperfect world the 'right' choice is sometimes the lesser of two evils. (Church of England)

In an imperfect world there will be circumstances where termination of a pregnancy may be the lesser of two evils. (Methodist Church)

More liberal Christians may argue that:
- Jesus taught his followers to act with a spirit of love and compassion.
- If the sanctity of life can be broken in war, perhaps it may be in abortion too.

- Life may not begin at conception.
- Some Catholics may argue that people should be able to use their free will to make choices about abortion, even though the Vatican forbids it.

Muslim attitudes to abortion

- There is some disagreement among Muslim scholars about when life begins: although most claim 120 days, some claim as early as 40 days, some when there is movement of the foetus.
- The most common view is that before 120 days a foetus that suffers from a serious, untreatable defect or a genetic blood disorder may be aborted.
- All Muslims accept that abortion can be permitted if the mother's life is in danger, and this is the only reason why it can take place after 120 days (after which, Muslims believe, the soul enters the body). The later the abortion, the greater the wrong.
- Different schools of Muslim thought have varying views on whether there are any other permitted reasons for abortion and when they may take place.
- Some schools of Muslim law allow abortion in the first 16 weeks of pregnancy, others only in the first 7 weeks.
- Muslims believe that abortion is wrong and haram (forbidden) but may be allowed in some cases, and it is not a punishable act.
- The Qur'an does not give any specific teaching on abortion but guidance on related matters is used to help decision making.
- Some Muslim scholars permit abortion when the mother has been raped or the foetus is the result of incest, but others still claim this is not permitted. No abortion is permitted if the woman commits adultery through her free choice or if the pregnancy is simply inconvenient to her.

In pre-Islamic Arabia, unwanted newborn babies, usually female children, were buried face down in the sand to suffocate. This was forbidden in the Qur'an, which also teaches that on Judgement Day aborted babies will call their mothers to account for why they were aborted: 'When the souls are sorted out, when the female infant buried alive is asked for what crime she was killed…when the world on high is unveiled…then shall each soul know what it has sent ahead' (Surah 81:7–9, 11, 14).

Muslims also believe that the principle of the sanctity of life is very important, and the Qur'an says: 'Whosoever has spared the life of a soul, it is as though he has spared the life of all people. Whosoever has killed a soul, it is as though he has murdered all of mankind' (Qur'an 5:32). However, when a mother's life is in danger, abortion is the lesser of two evils because:
- If the mother dies, in most cases the foetus will die anyway.
- The mother has responsibilities and is an existing part of a family.

However, an abortion should never take place because the family fears it cannot afford to have a child: 'Kill not your offspring for fear of poverty; it is we who provide for them and for you. Surely, killing them is a great sin' (Qur'an 17:32).

Key words

Abortion — the termination of the life of the foetus in the womb

Sanctity of life — the belief that life is created by God and made holy by him

Test yourself

1. Do you think there are any changes in the abortion law that should be made? Explain the reasons for your views.

2. Do you think that doctors should be obliged to carry out legal abortions even if they are opposed to abortion themselves? Explain the reasons for your view.

3. 'A woman should always have the right to an abortion — it is her body.' Do you agree? Give reasons.

4. Explain why you think that many women may be reluctant to carry their baby to full term for adoption and choose abortion instead.

5. Explain whether you think these are good reasons for having an abortion:
   a. The baby is going to have six fingers on each hand.
   b. The baby is going to be severely mentally handicapped and is not likely to live beyond 3 years of age.
   c. The mother is 12 years old.
   d. The mother already has two children, of whom one is has profound deafness and one has learning difficulties.

6. What do Christians understand by the sanctity of life and how does it affect beliefs about abortion?

7. Do you think that Christian or Muslim beliefs about abortion should have any influence on UK abortion law?

8. How might a Christian or Muslim respond to the claim that sometimes an abortion is the lesser of two evils?

Examination question

a. **What is an abortion?** (2 marks)

b. **Do you agree that there are justifiable reasons to permit abortion? Give two reasons for your view.** (6 marks)

c. **Why do Christians or Muslims have different beliefs about abortion?** (8 marks)

d. **'Every unborn child has the right to life.'**
   i. **Do you agree? Give reasons for your view.** (3 marks)
   ii. **Give reasons why some people may disagree with you.** (3 marks)

Exam tip

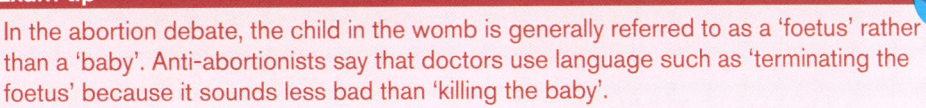

In the abortion debate, the child in the womb is generally referred to as a 'foetus' rather than a 'baby'. Anti-abortionists say that doctors use language such as 'terminating the foetus' because it sounds less bad than 'killing the baby'.

Topic 14
Euthanasia

Euthanasia literally means 'good death' and refers to the action of inducing a quiet and easy death. It is most often used to refer to the termination of the lives of people suffering from great physical or mental handicap or a painful terminal illness.

- **Voluntary euthanasia** is carried out at the request of the patient. It is this type of euthanasia that would most likely be legalised in the UK if many of the moral concerns about it were satisfactorily resolved.
- **Non-voluntary euthanasia** is carried out against the patient's wishes. This is the most controversial type of euthanasia.
- **Assisted suicide** occurs when someone helps a patient to end his or her life.
- Active euthanasia is carried out by a doctor performing a deliberate action, such as a lethal injection, to end the patient's life.
- Passive euthanasia is carried out when medical treatment or life support is deliberately withdrawn or when a severely ill or handicapped baby is not given treatment that would enable it to survive.

Those who support euthanasia offer the following reasons:

Arguments in favour of euthanasia

- It may be that the only way to ease a person's pain is by giving huge doses of painkillers that, in the end, cause death anyway. Sometimes this is done deliberately — such treatment is an example of double effect
- It allows the sufferer to die with dignity and avoids a slow death where the person's physical and mental condition may increasingly deteriorate, causing considerable suffering
- Supporters of euthanasia argue that people should not fear death, or see it as something evil and to be avoided
- It relieves the burden on families who might otherwise have to go to great trouble and expense
- It saves on hospital and medical expenses and allows more beds to be freed for non-terminal patients
- It leads to a gentle, pain-free death

50 GCSE Revision Guide

Even though human death is an evil to be fought against, and a reality which can never be sought intentionally, it may also at times be accepted, even welcomed, as a sign of God's mercy. (John Wyatt, Matters of Life and Death, 1998)

In some countries, most notably the Netherlands and Switzerland, euthanasia has been made legal under strict conditions. Here, supporters of euthanasia have claimed that all individuals have a human right to control their life, including the right to control their death.

In the UK the Voluntary Euthanasia Society has campaigned for people to be given the right to make living wills or advance directives indicating that, should they become severely injured or handicapped, they will be allowed to die rather than receive intensive medical treatment.

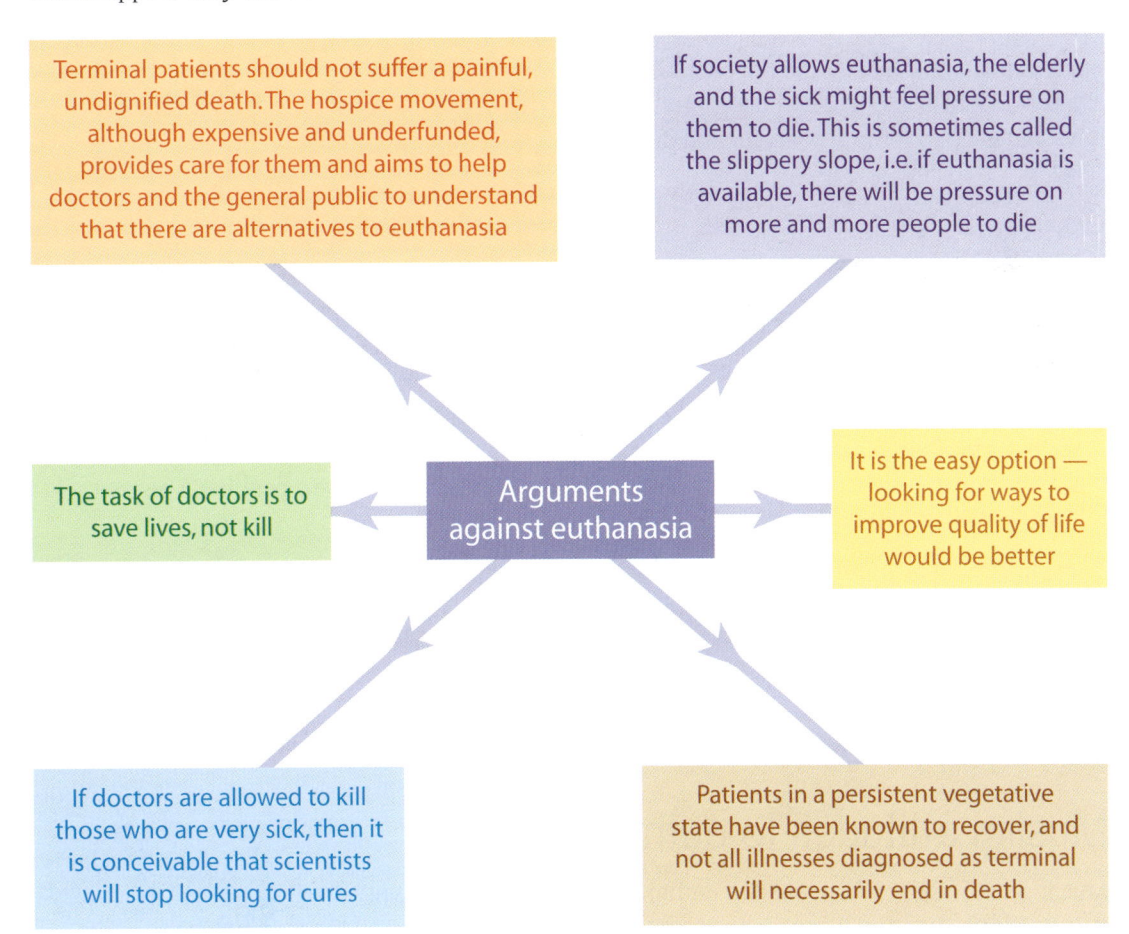

Arguments against euthanasia

- Terminal patients should not suffer a painful, undignified death. The hospice movement, although expensive and underfunded, provides care for them and aims to help doctors and the general public to understand that there are alternatives to euthanasia
- If society allows euthanasia, the elderly and the sick might feel pressure on them to die. This is sometimes called the slippery slope, i.e. if euthanasia is available, there will be pressure on more and more people to die
- The task of doctors is to save lives, not kill
- It is the easy option — looking for ways to improve quality of life would be better
- If doctors are allowed to kill those who are very sick, then it is conceivable that scientists will stop looking for cures
- Patients in a persistent vegetative state have been known to recover, and not all illnesses diagnosed as terminal will necessarily end in death

Christian attitudes to euthanasia

- Like abortion, euthanasia involves the issue of the sanctity of life.
- Most Christian churches are against euthanasia because life is regarded as a gift from God, which only he can take away.
- The Roman Catholic Church teaches that it is wrong to take (or fail to take) any action, medical or otherwise, that is intended to kill a patient, even if it is to relieve suffering.

An act or omission which causes death in order to eliminate suffering constitutes a murder greatly contrary to the dignity of the human person and to the respect due to the living God, his Creator. (*Catechism of the Catholic Church*)

We believe that it is right to use medical treatment to control pain. We deny the right to legalise the termination of life by a doctor. (The Salvation Army)

- It is taking away the life of a human being, which is always murder.
- Life is so valuable it should be valued even when someone is in great pain; no one should be able to make a judgement about the value of another person's life.
- Terminally ill patients can still worship God and show other people God's love.
- People should not value themselves so little that they think it would be better to die.

Many Christians consider the hospice movement to be an alternative to euthanasia. A hospice is a residential home where those suffering from terminal illness can live out their remaining days being cared for in a peaceful and dignified way.

We are now always able to control pain in terminal cancer in the patients sent to us… euthanasia as advocated is wrong…it should be unnecessary and is an admission of defeat. (Christian Hospice Movement)

However, some Christians are prepared to consider euthanasia under some circumstances:
- 'Even though human death…can never be sought intentionally, it may also at times be accepted, even welcomed, as a sign of God's mercy.' (John Wyatt, *Matters of Life and Death*, 1998)
- God intends that humans should have a good **quality of life** and, for some Christians, the principle of the sanctity of life allows for this.
- Euthanasia may be the most loving act for some patients and a way to genuinely respect their wishes and their dignity as individuals made in God's image.

For some Christians, the issue highlights the importance of preparing for death, which may include:
- providing advanced pain relief
- supporting the dying and those close to them
- being honest about death
- trusting the person's future to God

Muslim attitudes to euthanasia

Muslims are in general opposed to euthanasia on the grounds that:
- Human life is sacred because it is given by Allah and therefore all life is valuable.
- Allah alone chooses how long each person will live and human beings should not interfere in this.
- Euthanasia and suicide are not permitted in Islam.
- All suffering is a test, and the pain of illness must be faithfully endured.
- Rejecting suffering could have serious consequences for the afterlife.
- Taking care of the sick and old is pleasing to Allah.

The Qur'an teaches: 'When their time comes they cannot delay it for a single hour nor can they bring it forward by a single hour' (16:61).

The Islamic Code of Medical Ethics states:

Mercy killing, like suicide, finds no support except in the atheistic way of thinking that believes that our life on this earth is followed by void (nothingness). The claim of killing for painful, hopeless, illness is also refuted, for there is no human pain that cannot be largely conquered by medication or by suitable neurosurgery...

The strictest Muslim view is that all types of euthanasia are forbidden, based on the principle of maqasid ash-Sharia'ah (the preservation of life) and hifdh ad-din (preserving religion).

- 'Destroy not yourselves. Surely Allah is ever merciful to you' (Qur'an 4:29).
- 'If anyone kills a person — unless it be for murder or spreading mischief in the land — it would be as if he killed the whole people (Qur'an 5:32).'

The principle of hardship — mashaqqah — allows the law to be relaxed in some circumstances in order to relieve suffering, but the case of terminal illness is not among them.

> **Key words**
>
> **Assisted suicide** — helping a patient to commit suicide
>
> **Euthanasia** — good death — ending the life of a sick person in order to give release from pain
>
> **Non-voluntary euthanasia** — ending life against the person's wishes
>
> **Quality of life** — the value given to life depending on how far a person can find enjoyment and pleasure from it
>
> **Voluntary euthanasia** — ending life at the patient's own request

Test yourself

1. Should doctors be forced to abide by the wishes of a patient who asks to die? Explain your answer.

2. Who do you think should be involved in a patient's or doctor's decision to carry out euthanasia? For example, a partner, parent, friend, religious leader? Explain the reasons for your answer.

3. In 1993, the House of Lords rejected a proposal to legalise euthanasia, saying: 'It would be next to impossible to ensure that all acts of euthanasia were truly voluntary.' Do you think this is a genuine concern? Should it prevent the legalisation of euthanasia in the UK?

4. Search the internet for information about people who have travelled to Switzerland from the UK to die at the Dignitas clinic. Give your views on their cases and whether you think their decision was the best one for them.

5. What is the difference between sanctity of life and quality of life? Are they inevitably opposed to each other?

6. What does it mean to say that euthanasia may sometimes be the most loving thing to do?

7. List the main arguments in Islam concerning euthanasia. Which are the most and least convincing and why?

8 Muslims do allow a terminal patient to choose not to continue with medical treatment if it is causing hardship and doing so relieves patient and family of suffering.
Is this effectively the same as permitting euthanasia? Explain your answer.

Examination question

a **What is assisted suicide?** *(2 marks)*

b **Do you agree that euthanasia should never be permitted? Give two reasons for your view.** *(6 marks)*

c **Why do Christians have different beliefs about euthanasia?** *(8 marks)*

d **'A civilised society should allow its citizens to choose when to die.'**
   i **Do you agree? Give reasons for your view.** *(3 marks)*
   ii **Give reasons why some people may disagree with you.** *(3 marks)*

Topic 15
Matters of life and death in the media

It is important that matters of life and death are discussed in the media because:
- people need to know how the law may change over issues such as abortion and euthanasia
- issues of life and death affect everyone and people feel very strongly about them
- opinions are very divided and it is important we know how people think differently and discuss different views openly

Forms of media

There are several forms of media that allow these issues to be presented to the public:

How the media present matters of life and death

- **Newspapers** — have different styles of presentation and can indicate their own opinions on possible changes in the law
- **Television news** — daily programmes that may include special features on life and death issues
- **Television documentaries** — offer the opportunity to focus on a major issue at length, identifying different positions on the issue
- **Films** — use a detailed plot to examine an issue in depth, often based on a novel that has already introduced this idea to a smaller audience
- **Soap operas** — use changing storylines to examine issues in depth in a way that is accessible to the general public

Soap operas

Soap operas are long-running serials concerned with everyday life in which several storylines are carried over from one episode to the next. Regular events in soap operas include issues of family and relationships, but also issues such as abortion, euthanasia, and dealing with illness and death. If a particularly emotional issue has been addressed by a soap, then a helpline phone number is often displayed at the end, so people who have been affected by the issues can get support or extra information.

Newspapers

Newspapers can present matters of life and death and are not limited by plot lines or characters, since they can draw on the general public for different opinions and report what is happening all over the world at the same time. Each newspaper will usually have a characteristic way of dealing with issues, depending on its target readership and, while some may offer an opinion, others will appear to be unbiased. Contributions from medical, legal, or academic experts will contribute to their articles.

Films and documentaries

In most cases the moral theme of a film is presented alongside the more usual themes of popular film — romance, family dramas, adventures or fantasy — because most films are designed to entertain as well as inform. A director who wants simply to educate the audience about an issue of life or death will produce a documentary rather than a feature film. Many useful documentaries on television that cover issues of life and death (such as rare illnesses or disabilities, or the cases of individuals who have to make difficult choices) may often not reach a wide public audience.

Test yourself

1. Have a look at this week's newspapers. How many stories are about matters of life and death?

2. In the same way, watch the television news. Explain how it deals with issues of life and death. Are there any differences between the two? Give reasons.

3. Do you think television soaps and other programmes handle issues of life and death well or badly? Say why, using examples from television.

4. Do films and documentaries show life and death in greater detail than newspapers and television do?

5. In feature films the director may choose to focus the whole film on a moral issue. Should the director be unbiased, or rather present a whole range of opinions on an issue for viewers to discuss and consider?

6. Write a short review of a film you have seen that dealt with matters of life and death. Give your opinion on how well or badly the subject was treated and whether it was accurate and fair.

7. 'There should be no news censorship. Television and newspapers should show things exactly as they happen.' Do you agree? Give reasons for your view.

Marriage and family

Topic 16
Changing attitudes towards marriage, divorce, family and homosexuality

In the UK, attitudes towards marriage, divorce, the family and homosexuality have changed a great deal in the last 50 years.

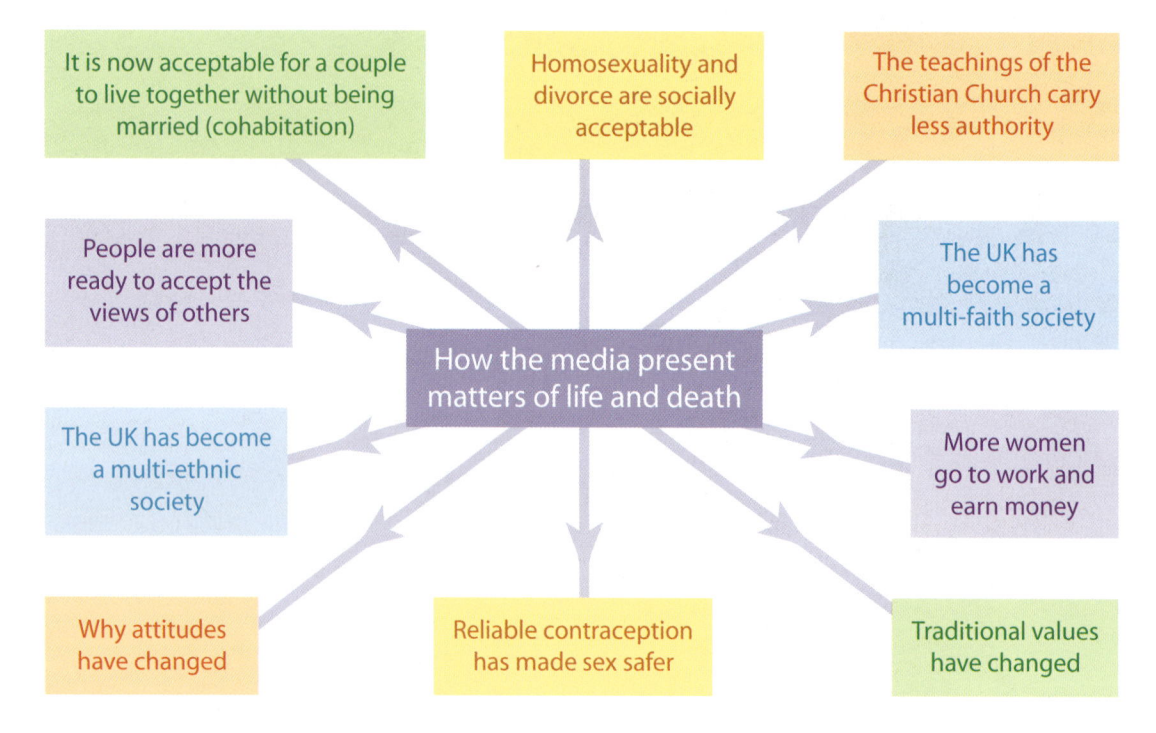

- It is now acceptable for a couple to live together without being married (cohabitation)
- Homosexuality and divorce are socially acceptable
- The teachings of the Christian Church carry less authority
- People are more ready to accept the views of others
- The UK has become a multi-faith society
- The UK has become a multi-ethnic society
- More women go to work and earn money
- Why attitudes have changed
- Reliable contraception has made sex safer
- Traditional values have changed

How the media present matters of life and death

How are attitudes changing?

Marriage

Marriage is the legal union of two people. In the UK fewer people are getting married and more couples are choosing to live together (**cohabitation**). For instance:

	Marriages
1972	480,000
2006	275,000

Divorce

Divorce is the legal termination of a marriage. Approximately one third of marriages end in divorce.

	Divorces
1981	145,000
2004	153,000

One third of marriages end in divorce

Families

Family life is still the way most people live, with 20 million people in the UK in a traditional family set-up of parents and children living together. However, more children, about 42%, are born to parents who are not married.

Homosexuality

Homosexuality has become much more socially acceptable and homosexuals are protected by law from discrimination and abuse. The 2005 Civil Partnership Act legally recognised same-sex **civil partnerships** and some same-sex couples have pursued their right to have a biologically related child.

Key words

Civil partnerships — give same-sex couples the same legal rights and protection as a civil marriage

Cohabitation — living together without being married

Divorce — the legal termination of a marriage

Homosexuality — sexual attraction to people of the same gender

Test yourself

1 Explain the meaning of the following terms:
   a cohabitation
   b divorce
   c homosexuality
   d marriage
   e family

2 What is the meaning of the following quotations and what problems may be raised by each of them?

   'It is good for a man not to marry' (1 Corinthians 7:1)

   'Do not lie with a man as one lies with a woman; that is detestable' (Leviticus 18:22).

3 Why has the availability of contraception had an effect on the way we think about relationships?

4 Why are fewer people getting married today than in the past?

5 Why do many marriages end in divorce?

Examination question

Why do you think people are more tolerant today of homosexuality?

Exam tip
Although the UK does not allow homosexual marriages, there are a number of churches that are prepared to give a Service of Blessing on long-term homosexual relationships.

Topic 17
Christian attitudes to sex outside marriage

The Christian Church teaches that sex is an act of love and commitment and should take place only in marriage. Christians, therefore, are urged not to have sex before being married (**pre-marital sex**) and not to have sex with someone if they are already married to someone else (**adultery**). Christians must avoid having casual sexual relationships (**promiscuity**) and married couples should show **faithfulness** to each other.

Biblical teaching on sex outside marriage

Here is what the Bible says. What do you think?

- 'God wants you to be holy and completely free from sexual immorality' (1 Thessalonians 4:3)
- 'You shall not commit adultery' (Exodus 20:14)
- 'Do you not know that your body is a temple of the Holy Spirit?' (1 Corinthians 6:18)
- 'Anyone who looks at a woman lustfully has already committed adultery with her in his heart' (Matthew 5:28)
- 'The wife's body does not belong to her alone, but also to her husband. In the same way, the husband's body does not belong to him alone but also to his wife' (1 Corinthians 7:4)

What the Bible says

Some Christians today believe that cohabitation (living together without being married) should be allowed as a 'trial marriage'. They say that this can lead to a better and more lasting relationship with their partner.

The Silver Ring Thing

Christian organisations such as 'The Silver Ring Thing' have been set up to help and support young people who do not want to have sex before marriage. Young people pay £20 and wear a special ring, showing that they are committed to not having sex before marriage.

Religious Studies

Other Christian views

Many Christians today feel that sex before marriage is right if the couple love each other and are in a long-term relationship and intend to get married to each other in the future. They believe that the teaching of the Bible is old-fashioned and that forbidding sex before marriage can ruin a loving relationship.

> **Key words**
>
> **Adultery** — having sex with someone when you are already married to someone else
>
> **Faithfulness** — staying loyal to your marriage partner and having sex with no one else
>
> **Pre-marital sex** — having sex with someone before you are married
>
> **Promiscuity** — having casual sexual relationships

Test yourself

1. Here are some of the reasons why many Christians are opposed to sex outside marriage. Do you agree or disagree with them? Why?
   - The Bible allows for sex only between marriage partners.
   - Children born outside marriage may have a less stable family life.
   - Promiscuity makes a person vulnerable to sexually transmitted infections.
   - Loving sexual relations unite a married couple together.
   - Adultery breaks the marriage vow of faithfulness.

2. Explain the meaning of the following terms:
   - faithfulness
   - promiscuity
   - pre-marital sex
   - adultery

3. Outline the meaning of the following quotations and consider one problem that may be raised by each of them:
   - 'Anyone who divorces his wife and marries another woman commits adultery' (Mark 10:11).
   - 'Sex is only for bringing more children into the world.'

4. What are the arguments for and against sex outside marriage?

5. Do you think that cohabitation is a good or bad thing? Why?

6. Do you think that organisations such as 'The Silver Ring Thing' should be encouraged or discouraged? Why?

Examination question

Explain why Christians have different views on sex outside marriage.

> **Exam tip**
>
> In 1995, the Church of England published a report called 'Something to celebrate', which offered support to the notion of cohabitation.

Topic 18
Muslim attitudes to sex outside marriage

The teachings of the Qur'an

For Muslims, sex outside marriage is wrong.

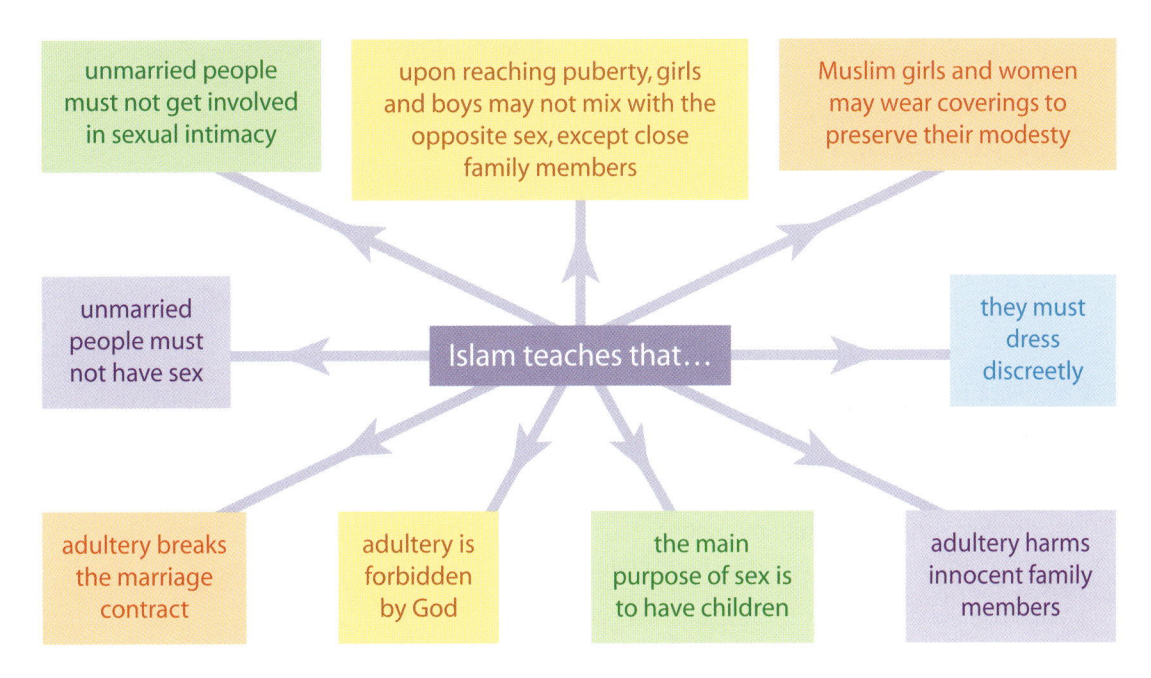

Islam teaches that…

- unmarried people must not get involved in sexual intimacy
- upon reaching puberty, girls and boys may not mix with the opposite sex, except close family members
- Muslim girls and women may wear coverings to preserve their modesty
- unmarried people must not have sex
- they must dress discreetly
- adultery breaks the marriage contract
- adultery is forbidden by God
- the main purpose of sex is to have children
- adultery harms innocent family members

What is your opinion of these teachings? Why?

This also means that Muslims should not cohabit with a partner outside marriage. Indeed, all Muslims are expected to get married. The reasons for this are:
- The Prophet Muhammad was married.
- Marriage brings God's blessing and forgiveness.
- Sexual desire is a gift of new life from God and is fulfilled through marriage.

Muslims tend to marry other Muslims and often at quite a young age. The ideal marriage partner is one who loves God. In some Islamic countries, Muslim men may have more than one marriage partner. This is called polygamy. The maximum number of wives a man can usually have is four.

Religious Studies

Honour killings

On very rare occasions, a Muslim who has had sex outside marriage may be murdered. This is called an 'honour killing' and occurs where family members kill the 'offender' because it is believed that the person has dishonoured the family. Although this is against Muslim teaching, in the UK there are several such murders every year, usually performed by male members of a family against a female member who has, for example, had sex outside marriage. In 2003, Heshu Yones, aged 16, was murdered by her father because he believed she had dishonoured the family with her Western lifestyle and Christian boyfriend. The father was sentenced to life imprisonment.

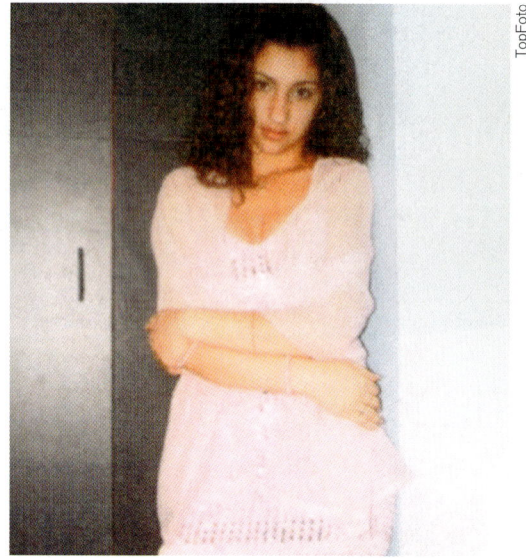

Heshu Yones

Test yourself

1 What is your opinion of the views expressed in the following quotations?
   – 'Adultery is sinful.'
   – 'Honour killings are simply murder.'
   – 'People should be allowed to have as many husbands/wives as they want to.'
   – 'Women should always be veiled in public places.'

2 Here are some of the reasons why many Muslims are opposed to sex outside marriage. Do you agree or disagree with them? Why?
   – It is forbidden by God.
   – It breaks the marriage contract.
   – It harms innocent family members.
   – The main purpose of sex is to have children.

3 What are the arguments for and against polygamy?

4 Why do Muslims consider adultery to be a sin?

5 Why are Muslims encouraged to dress discreetly?

Examination question

Explain why most Muslims are opposed to sex outside marriage.

Exam tip
Adultery and promiscuity are not against the law in the UK. In Islamic countries that operate under the Shari'ah law, they are, in some cases, punishable by death.

Topic 19
Christian attitudes to divorce

A divorce is the legal termination of a marriage and in the UK about a third of marriages end in divorce. Divorce is allowed when a marriage has 'irretrievably broken down'. This is usually shown by:

Adultery — where one partner has sex with someone other than the marriage partner

Causes of irretrievable breakdown of marriage

Unreasonable behaviour — where one partner continually behaves very badly towards the other

Desertion — where one partner leaves the other

The marriage of Sir Paul McCartney and Heather Mills ended in divorce

Key words
Re-marriage — marrying again after being divorced from an earlier marriage

Religious Studies

The Christian viewpoint

Christians have differing views about whether or not it is right for believers to get divorced:

- marriage is a sacred promise made before God that should not be broken
- Jesus said that divorce was wrong
- marriage is a sacrament — a holy action that brings a person closer to God

The Roman Catholic Church does not allow divorce because…

NB Sometimes an annulment is granted — a declaration by the Church that a true/lawful marriage did not take place

- a Roman Catholic who does divorce cannot re-marry in a Roman Catholic Church
- 'Marriage cannot be dissolved by any human power or for any reason other than death' (*Catechism of the Catholic Church*)

- Jesus seemed to allow for divorce in the case of unfaithfulness
- Human beings can make mistakes and relationships do break down
- God is always ready to forgive sins
- Divorced people are allowed to re-marry in a Protestant Church

The Protestant Church allows divorce in certain circumstances because…

- 'Marriage should always be undertaken as a lifelong commitment but that there are circumstances in which a divorced person may be married in church' (Church of England statement on marriage)
- With God's forgiveness, believers may divorce and find happiness with a different marriage partner

GCSE Revision Guide

Test yourself

1. Do you agree or disagree with the views expressed below? Say why.

   'People should live together before they get married.'

   'Marriage should be for life.'

   'Anyone who divorces his wife and marries another woman commits adultery against her.'

   'It is too easy to get a divorce — it should be made much more difficult.'

   'A couple who marry in church are less likely to divorce.'

   'Divorce should be allowed only for unfaithfulness.'

2. What is the meaning of the following words:
   - sacrament
   - annulment
   - re-marriage?

Examination question

a **What is re-marriage?** (2 marks)

b **Do you think being divorced is better than being unhappily married? Give two reasons for your view.** (6 marks)

c **Why do some Christians support allowing divorce and some do not?** (8 marks)

d **'Anyone can make a mistake — divorce should be allowed for Christians.'**
   i Do you agree? Give reasons for your view. (3 marks)
   ii Give reasons why some people may disagree with you. (3 marks)

Exam tip
The teaching of Jesus concerning divorce is not clear. In Mark 10:11-12 he prohibits divorce, but in Matthew 5:32 Jesus appears to allow divorce on grounds of marital unfaithfulness.

Topic 20
Muslim attitudes to divorce

When Muslims may divorce

- If one partner leaves Islam
- If one partner is absent for a very long time
- Refusing to care for the partner
- Refusing to have sexual relations

Muslims may divorce only under strict conditions

- If one partner is in prison for a long time
- For any other reason, the husband announces three times over a period of 3 months his intention to divorce his wife
- Where there is unfaithfulness and adultery

Muslims may only divorce under strict conditions

GCSE Revision Guide

The Iddah

The 'Iddah' is the waiting period — the time between the couple splitting up and the divorce being granted. It is an important time because it gives the couple an opportunity to mend their relationship.

If the husband and wife are divorced, they are free to re-marry. The husband remains financially responsible for his ex-wife and their children until she remarries.

Muslim families will try to help couples who face divorce. Islamic teaching on divorce is designed to encourage the couple to settle their differences peacefully and, if possible, get back together. However, is not designed to force unhappy couples to stay together. If this is clearly impossible, the law allows a quick and easy divorce.

Test yourself

1 Explain the reasons why Muslims may have different views about divorce.
2 Make a list of the grounds upon which a Muslim couple may divorce.

Examination question

a **What is a divorce?** (2 marks)

b **Do you think that the Muslim divorce rules are fair? Give two reasons for your view.** (6 marks)

c **Explain the main differences between Muslim and Christian divorce rules.** (8 marks)

d **'A Muslim should never divorce'**
  i **Do you agree? Give reasons for your opinion.** (3 marks)
  ii **Give reasons why some people may disagree with you.** (3 marks)

Exam tip
One of the greatest emphases in marriage in Islam is on faithfulness — the belief that, once married, a couple should be committed sexually and emotionally to each other.

Topic 21
Christian teachings on family life

Most Christians are supporters of marriage and believe that it is the best setting for the bringing of children into the world (**procreation**). They believe that children should be brought up in a loving family environment because they are a gift from God and that parents have special responsibilities towards their children. In the same way, as children grow up, they have responsibilities towards their parents.

The family is the community in which, from childhood, one can learn moral values, begin to honour God and make good use of freedom. (Catechism of the Catholic Church)

Marriage is given, that husband and wife...may have children and be blessed in caring for them and bringing them up in accordance with God's will. (Church of England, Alternative Service Book)

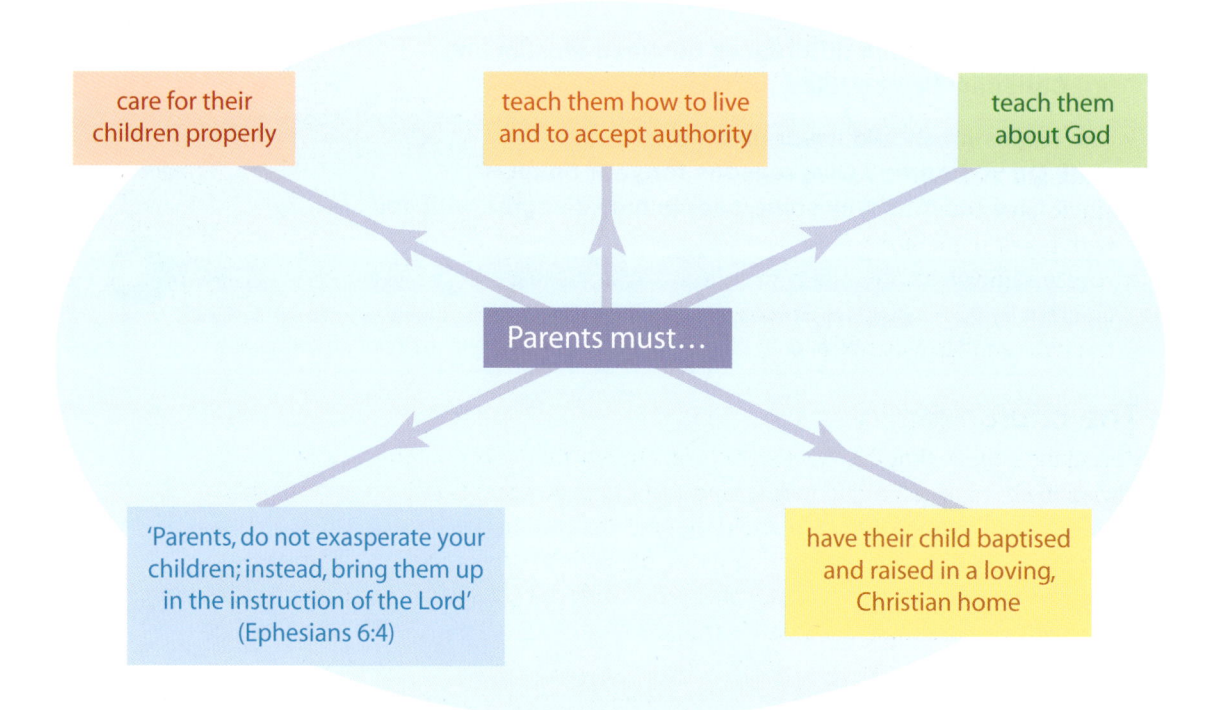

Parents must...

- care for their children properly
- teach them how to live and to accept authority
- teach them about God
- 'Parents, do not exasperate your children; instead, bring them up in the instruction of the Lord' (Ephesians 6:4)
- have their child baptised and raised in a loving, Christian home

Children must…
- obey their parents until they are adults themselves
- respect their parents
- care for their parents when they grow old
- 'Honour your father and your mother' (Exodus 20:12)
- 'Children, obey your parents' (Ephesians 6:1)

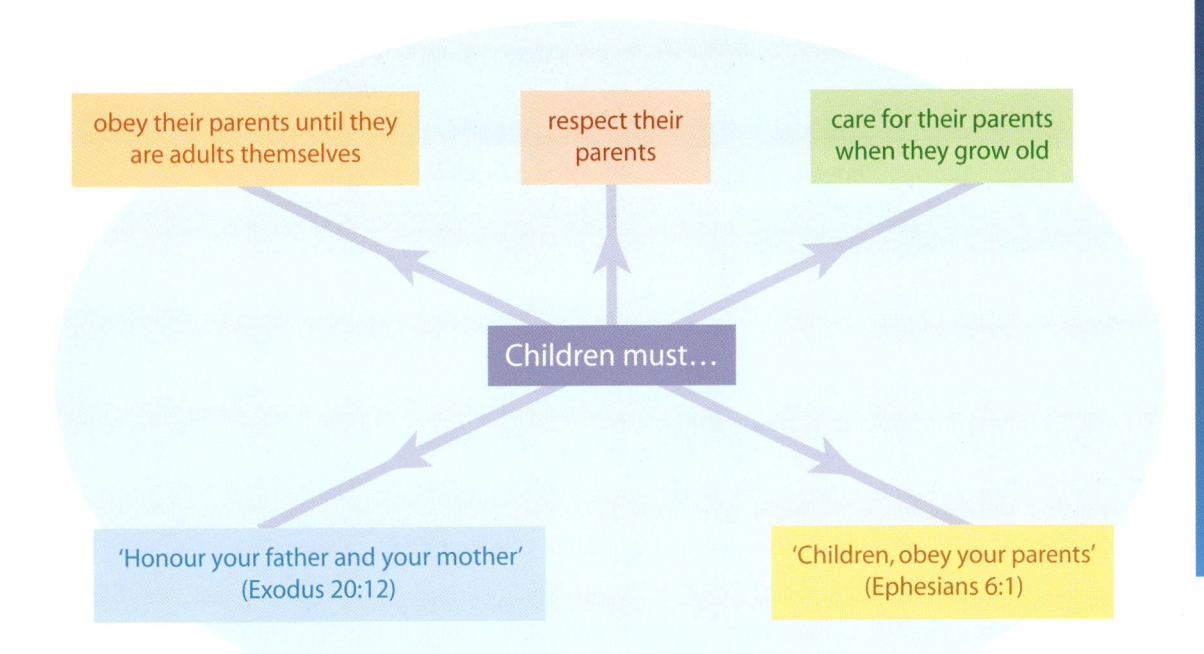

Types of family

There are different types of family:
- **nuclear family** — two parents and their children all living together
- extended family — where parents, children and other relatives live together
- single-parent family — one parent living alone with his or her children
- **re-constituted family** — where a couple with children by previous marriages join together and the two families become one

A nuclear family — two parents and their children living together

The church family

Christians believe that the members of the church should be united like a family. Christian churches offer help and support to Christian parents to help them to raise their children in a loving family environment. They do this by:
- baptising children and welcoming them into the Christian faith and community
- helping Christian parents to educate their children through Sunday schools and youth groups where young people can learn about God
- running Church schools that educate children in a Christian environment
- holding family services on Sundays, and special services at Christmas, Easter and Harvest

A number of Christian organisations exist to help families in times of particular difficulty. For example:
- The Children's Society
- National Children's Homes
- The Catholic Marriage Advisory Council
- The Child Welfare Council
- The Methodist Homes for the Aged

> **Key words**
>
> **Nuclear family** — two parents and their children all living together
>
> **Procreation** — having children
>
> **Re-constituted family** — where two adults with children join together to become one family

Test yourself

1 What do you think the following quotations mean?
 – 'Honour your father and your mother.'
 – 'Parents, do not exasperate your children.'
 – 'Grown children have responsibilities towards their parents.'

2 List the **three** most important teachings that adult Christians follow concerning family life. Why are these so important?

3 What are the main principles that a child should follow when being brought up by Christian parents?

4 Explain **three** ways in which the Church can help to support Christian families.

5 Why do you think that the Bible does not require children to love their parents?

6 Do you think that Church schools are a good or bad thing?

Examination question

a **What is procreation?** (2 marks)

b **Explain how being a Christian might help a couple to raise their children. Give two reasons for your view.** (6 marks)

c **Explain why some Christians believe that being married is such an important part of family life.** (8 marks)

d **'Family life is more important for religious people than non-religious people.'**
 i **Do you agree? Give reasons for your opinion.** (3 marks)
 ii **Give reasons why some people may disagree with you.** (3 marks)

> **Exam tip**
>
> The fastest-growing type of family today is the single-parent family. This is because of the increase in the divorce rate and because more women are choosing to have a child without a permanent partner.

Topic 22
Muslim teachings on family life

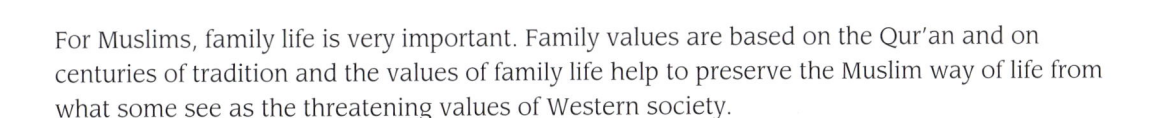

For Muslims, family life is very important. Family values are based on the Qur'an and on centuries of tradition and the values of family life help to preserve the Muslim way of life from what some see as the threatening values of Western society.

For Muslims, family life…
- provides a secure and encouraging environment for parents and children
- is the best way of raising children in the Islamic faith
- provides protection against wrongful sexual desires and relationships
- helps to develop qualities such as love, kindness, mercy and compassion
- discourages antisocial behaviour
- encourages individuals to see themselves as part of a wider community

The Muslim family

Muslim families often include not only parents and children, but also other relatives. The raising of children in the Islamic faith is very important and follows clear guidelines:
- The mother takes responsibility for the religious upbringing of her children.
- The beliefs and values of Islam, including the principles of haram (forbidden) and halal (permitted), are learned in the family.
- Parents are responsible for sending their children to the madrasah, an Islamic place of learning where Muslim children can learn to read the Qur'an in Arabic.
- Some Muslim parents may choose to send their children to Muslim schools.

A Muslim marriage ceremony

Religious Studies

- Within the mosque the imam may offer advice on all matters of marriage.
- Families in financial need may get help from the zakah fund.

Muslims and marriage

All Muslims are encouraged to marry and stay faithful. Being married is seen to increase the value of a person's prayers, and brings God's power, blessing and forgiveness. Also, men and women are encouraged through marriage to fulfil their sexual desires and to have children.

Today, most Muslims will choose their own marriage partners, though some Muslim marriages will be arranged by a couple's parents. Most Muslims will marry other Muslims and marriage is encouraged at a young age.

Muslims also believe that they are members of the worldwide family (ummah) of Islam.

Test yourself

1 What is the meaning of the following words:
  – haram
  – zakah
  – halal
  – ummah
  – madrasah

2 What are the main responsibilities of Muslim parents?

3 What are the main responsibilities of Muslim children?

4 How does Muslim teaching on the family differ from Christian teaching? Why do you think this is?

Examination question

a What is faithfulness? (2 marks)

b Explain how being a Muslim might help a couple to raise their children. Give two reasons for your view. (6 marks)

c Explain why Muslims believe that being married is such an important part of family life. (8 marks)

d 'Religious guidelines do not guarantee a happy family life.'
  i Do you agree? Give reasons for your opinion. (3 marks)
  ii Give reasons why some people may disagree with you. (3 marks)

Exam tip
These are religious traditions. In your answers, make sure that you know them properly — don't just guess what they are — and think carefully about what they mean, even if you do not agree with them.

Topic 23
Christian attitudes to homosexuality

Homosexuality is sexual attraction to members of one's own sex. In the UK, the age of consent for homosexual activity is 16. Homosexuals are not allowed to marry, but may enter into a civil partnership, which is a legal commitment between two members of the same sex.

Christians are divided in their views on homosexuality.

Christians who oppose homosexuality say it is against Christian teaching because…
- God created man and woman to be in a marriage relationship together
- two same-sex partners cannot have a child
- homosexuality is not good for society, as it undermines the family
- the Bible teaches against homosexuality: 'Do not lie with a man as one lies with a woman; that is detestable' (Leviticus 18:22)
- the New Testament says: 'Neither the sexually immoral…nor homosexual offenders will inherit the kingdom of God' (1 Corinthians 6:9–10)

Christians who support homosexuality say that…
- homosexual people are entitled to the same rights as everyone else
- homosexual people, too, are created by God
- homosexual people can be as loving and caring as heterosexual people

Religious Studies

Elton John and David Furnish entered into a civil partnership in 2005

Roman Catholic views on homosexuality

- The Roman Catholic Church recommends that homosexuals remain **celibate** (do not have active sexual relationships).
- Practising homosexuals may not act as priests in the Roman Catholic Church.
- Some Roman Catholics believe that homosexuality is a disorder and that Christians who are homosexual should pray to God to help them.

Protestant views on homosexuality

- Many Protestant Christians believe that homosexual relationships are not ideal, but are better than promiscuity.
- Some argue that the Church should fully accept homosexual partnerships.
- Homosexual partnerships should be judged on the strength of the love and commitment of the partners.
- 'There are circumstances in which individuals may justifiably choose to enter into a homosexual relationship with the hope of enjoying companionship and a physical expression of love similar to that found in marriage.' (Church of England Statement on Sexuality)

Key words

Celibacy — refraining from sexual activity for religious reasons

Test yourself

1. Do you agree or disagree with the following statements? Give reasons:
   - 'Homosexuals should be allowed to marry, just like everyone else.'
   - 'Homosexuality is wrong because the Bible says so.'
   - 'A gay priest can be just as good as a straight priest.'

2. What are the views of the Roman Catholic Church concerning homosexuality?

3. What are the views of the Protestant Church concerning homosexuality?

4. Which of these views do you agree with and why?

Examination question

a What is a civil partnership? *(2 marks)*

b Do you think the law regarding homosexuality is fair or not? Give two reasons for your view. *(6 marks)*

c Explain why some Christians support homosexuality and others do not. *(8 marks)*

d 'No Christian should be a practising homosexual.'
   i Do you agree? Give reasons for your opinion. *(3 marks)*
   ii Give reasons why some people may disagree with you. *(3 marks)*

Exam tip
Homosexuality is a very controversial area, concerning the meaning of biblical verses such as Leviticus 18:22 and 1 Corinthians 6:9. Make sure you know and understand their meaning.

Topic 24
Muslim attitudes to homosexuality

Although there are differing views, most Muslims are against homosexuality.

Muslims who oppose homosexuality say…

- it goes against Muslim traditions about the characteristics of men and women
- it is punishable by death under Shari'ah law
- in the Qur'an, the 'people of Lot' were destroyed by God for practising homosexuality
- it is a grave sin
- it is a threat to family life
- homosexuality is chosen, not natural
- it means fewer Muslim children are born
- it is not possible to be gay and be a Muslim
- it is harmful to the health of the individuals

The death penalty

Homosexuality carries the death penalty in several Muslim states including Saudi Arabia and Iran. Some estimate that more than 4,000 homosexuals have been executed in Iran since 1979. Although human rights groups such as Amnesty International condemn such punishments, most Muslim nations say that anti-homosexual laws are based on the Qur'an.

Protest against the deportation of Mehdi Kazemi to Iran, where homosexuality carries the death penalty

Muslim support for homosexuals

Some Muslims, such as Al-Fatiha, a Muslim homosexual rights group, offer support to homosexuals rather than let them be excluded from the Islamic community. They argue that:
- Homosexuality is natural.
- The teaching of the Qur'an is no longer relevant to the modern world.
- The Qur'an condemns homosexual lust and promiscuity but not homosexual love.

Test yourself

1 Do you agree or disagree with the following statements? Give reasons.

   'Homosexuality is a grave sin and should be punished by death.'

   'Homosexuality is chosen, not natural.'

   'Islamic teachings on homosexuality are out of date.'

   'There is no such thing as a gay Muslim.'

   'Homosexuality goes against the characteristics of men and women.'

2 Why is homosexuality regarded as harmful by Muslims?

3 Compare and contrast Muslim and Christian attitudes to homosexuality.

Examination question

a **What is homosexuality?** (2 marks)

b **Explain why some Muslims think that homosexuality is a threat to family life. Give two reasons for your view.** (6 marks)

c **Explain different Muslims attitudes to homosexuality.** (8 marks)

d **'No Muslim should be a practising homosexual.'**
   i **Do you agree? Give reasons for your opinion.** (3 marks)
   ii **Give reasons why some people may disagree with you.** (3 marks)

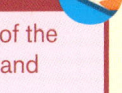

Exam tip
Homosexuality is a very controversial area for Muslims, concerning the meaning of the teachings of the Qur'an and Muslim traditions. Make sure you know and understand their meaning.

Topic 25
Christian attitudes to contraception

Contraception is the deliberate prevention of pregnancy by natural or artificial methods. It involves using one of a number of methods, including the pill, the coil, condoms and sterilisation. Christians are divided over the issue of whether or not to use contraception.

- every act of sexual intercourse should be open to the possibility of conception
- Many Christians, including most Roman Catholics, are opposed to the use of contraception because…
- God commanded people to 'Be fruitful and multiply' (Genesis 1:28)
- contraception prevents people from fulfilling God's command

Christians opposed to contraception

Some Christians who will not use contraception have families with ten or more children. They claim that children are a gift from God that should not be controlled by humans.

Those opposed to contraception believe that couples should use only a natural method of contraception — having sexual intercourse at the times in the woman's menstrual cycle when she is not likely to conceive.

Christians who support contraception

Christians who use contraception usually do so because they have decided that it is not appropriate for them to have children.

Marriage and family

```
they consider themselves too young or too old to have a child
becoming pregnant would be harmful to the health of the mother
they feel their lifestyle would not be compatible with having a child
they feel unable to provide financially or emotionally for a child
```
→ **Christians may choose to use contraception because…** ←
```
one or both partners carry a genetically inherited condition
they want to avoid spreading sexually-transmitted diseases
many Protestant churches support the use of contraception
```

Many Christians believe that the use of contraception within a marriage relationship is the right way to plan a family. For such Christians, the pill and condoms are acceptable because they prevent conception from taking place. However, some Christians will not use the coil or the morning after pill because they act after conception and are considered to be equivalent to an abortion, and are therefore unacceptable.

Key words

Contraception — the deliberate prevention of pregnancy by natural or artificial methods

Religious Studies

Test yourself

1 Give **three** reasons why some Christians are opposed to contraception.

2 Give **three** reasons why some Christians support the use of contraception.

3 Is having ten or more children accepting God's gift or acting irresponsibly?

4 Do we have the right to control birth by contraception? Why/why not?

Examination question

a **What is contraception?** (2 marks)

b **Do you think it is right to use contraception? Give two reasons for your view.** (6 marks)

c **Explain different Christian attitudes to contraception.** (8 marks)

d **'It is better to use contraception than to have an unwanted baby.'**
   i **Do you agree? Give reasons for your opinion.** (3 marks)
   ii **Give reasons why some people may disagree with you.** (3 marks)

Exam tip

Many Christians, including Roman Catholics, oppose the morning after pill and the coil because they act after conception has taken place — in other words, when a human life has actually begun.

Topic 26
Muslim attitudes to contraception

Among Muslims there are differing views on contraception.

Many Muslims on both sides agree that sterilisation and vasectomy are not acceptable if they are done to ensure that a married couple never have children at any stage in their marriage, since having children is an important part of Muslim life and duty.

While some Muslim countries are very strict and do not allow contraception to be freely available, other Muslim countries actively encourage the use of contraception among married couples and teach people about it at a young age.

Muslims believe that contraception should be used only in marriage and that the unmarried should not have sexual relationships (and therefore use contraception) before marriage.

Recent surveys show that there are more Muslim children being born than those of any other faith.

Muslim arguments against contraception

- Contraception can lead to promiscuity and adultery
- Children are a gift from God
- The coil and morning after pill cause a very early abortion
- The Qur'an states: 'You should not kill your children for fear of want' (17:31, 6:151)
- Contraception may prevent a woman from having sexual fulfilment

Religious Studies

Muslim arguments in favour of contraception

- It is permissible if the mother's life or health would be in danger if she became pregnant
- It can be used only for the well-being of the couple or the rest of the family
- Contraception makes a woman more attractive to her husband
- The right to use contraception frees women from male domination

Test yourself

1 Explain the reasons why some Muslims are opposed to contraception.

2 Explain why some Muslims are in favour of contraception.

3 What do you think the text 'You should not kill your children for fear of want' means?

4 Compare Christian and Muslim attitudes to contraception. Which attitudes do you most agree with and why?

Examination question

a **What is adultery?** *(2 marks)*

b **Do you think contraception leads to promiscuity? Give two reasons for your view.** *(6 marks)*

c **Explain different Muslim attitudes to contraception.** *(8 marks)*

d **'Contraception should be available only to married couples.' Do you agree? Give reasons for your opinion.** *(3 marks)*

Exam tip
For many Muslims, contraception is not as important an issue as, say, abortion. It is, arguably, a more controversial issue in Christianity.

Religion and community cohesion

Topic 27
Changing attitudes to gender roles

The changing roles of men and women

A century ago…

- most women stayed at home, cared for the house and looked after the children
- only 15% of married women went out to work
- women were not allowed to vote (up until 1918)
- most men went out to work to earn money to keep the family

Today…

- men are more willing to be involved in looking after the home
- many women go out to work
- more women are achieving great success in art, sport and business
- girls are achieving higher grades in examinations than boys
- men take an active role in bringing up their children
- the Equal Pay Act 1970 gives women equal pay with men
- the contraceptive pill has given women more freedom

Anita Roddick, founder of the Body Shop

Is there real equality?

However, there is not full **equality** — recent surveys have shown that:

- Men still earn around 17% more than women.
- Many women are in low-paid and traditionally female jobs such as nursing and in the caring professions.
- There are very few women in senior positions in large corporations.

There are many reasons for this inequality. Some problems are caused, it is claimed, by employers holding **sexist** attitudes and discriminating against women.

Also, some women take career breaks in order to bring up babies and young children, and then miss out on promotion opportunities when they return to work.

> **Key words**
>
> **Equality** — where everyone has equal rights
>
> **Sexism** — discriminating against people because of their gender

Test yourself

1. Explain the meaning of the following terms:
   - equality
   - sexism
   - discrimination

2. In two columns, list traditional attitudes towards gender roles and how those attitudes have changed today.

3. Identify **three** ways in which gender roles have changed in the UK in recent years.

4. With reference to each of the following statements, state whether you agree, giving your reasons and showing that you have considered other points of view:

   'A woman's place is in the home.'

   'A woman who does not reach the top of her profession has only herself to blame.'

   'Men should take a more active role in bringing up children.'

   'The contraceptive pill has given women more freedom.'

Religious Studies

Examination question

a What is sexism? *(2 marks)*

b Do you think that there is still sexual discrimination in the UK? Give two reasons for your view. *(6 marks)*

c Give reasons why some people support the idea of women staying at home to look after children and others do not. *(8 marks)*

d 'Passing laws against sexual discrimination will not lead to sexual equality.'
  i Do you agree? Give reasons for your view. *(3 marks)*
  ii Give reasons why some people may disagree with you. *(3 marks)*

Exam tip
In your answers try to consider how attitudes in the UK have changed over the last hundred years, but also try to think of reasons why traditional views are still strong.

Topic 28
Christian attitudes to equal rights for women

The teaching of the Bible

Christian teaching on the roles of men and women is controversial and not always clear.

In favour of equality, Christianity teaches that…

- men and women are created equal
- 'God created humankind in his own image… male and female, he created them' (Genesis 1:27)
- Jesus Christ treated all women with great respect
- Jesus had many women followers who learned from him

Against equality, Christianity teaches that…

- a woman is, most importantly, a wife and mother
- her first priority is to look after the home and care for the children
- 'Wives, submit to your husbands as to the Lord. For a husband has authority over his wife…' (Ephesians 5:21)
- Jesus's twelve disciples were all men

Religious Studies

Adam and Eve (Genesis 1–3)

These differing views may have come originally from the biblical story of Adam and Eve, the first humans. In the story, both live in the Garden of Eden but Eve is tempted to disobey God's command and she eats the forbidden fruit. Then she talks to Adam and he does likewise. As a result, their loving relationship with God is broken.

Some Christians believe that women are inferior because they are descendants of Eve, who, rather than Adam, was sinful:

For Adam was formed first, then Eve…it was the woman who was deceived and became a sinner. (1 Timothy 2:13–14)

However, other Christians believe that men and women are created equal by God and the Adam and Eve story is not about a sinful woman and an innocent man, but is the story of a couple who share their sin and punishment together, as well as sharing in God's love.

Women priests

One area of real Christian inequality today concerns women priests. The Roman Catholic Church does not allow women to become priests (ordination) and the Church of England has allowed women to become priests only in recent years. The main reason why women have not been allowed to become priests is the teaching of St Paul, who wrote:

Women should remain silent in churches. They are not allowed to speak, but must be in submission, as the Law says. (1 Corinthians 14:34)

Many Christians disagree with this teaching. They claim that women have particular skills that can make them exceptional priests, for instance, offering loving and sympathetic care to those in need. It is a controversial area and the arguments will continue for many years to come.

Only in recent years has the Church of England allowed women to become priests

Test yourself

1 Suggest how the story of Adam and Eve may be used to justify inequality and also to show equality between the sexes. Use two columns to show the inequalities and equalities.

2 Outline the meaning of the following quotations and consider one problem that may be raised by each of them:

'God created humankind in his own image… male and female, he created them' (Genesis 1:27).

'Wives, submit to your husbands as to the Lord. For the husband is the head of the wife as Christ is the head of the Church' (Ephesians 5:22).

'Women should remain silent in churches. They are not allowed to speak, but must be in submission, as the Law says' (1 Corinthians 14:34).

3 Suggest **three** arguments against ordaining women as priests, and three arguments in favour of it.

Examination question

a **What is inequality?** (2 marks)

b **Do you think that Christianity is sexist? Give two reasons for your view.** (6 marks)

c **Why do some Christians support equality between men and women and others do not?** (8 marks)

d **'Women are better equipped to become priests than men.'**
  i **Do you agree? Give reasons for your view.** (3 marks)
  ii **Give reasons why some people may disagree with you.** (3 marks)

Exam tip
Remember that this is about Christian attitudes. Make sure you refer to Christianity and Christian teachings in your answer.

Topic 29
Muslim attitudes towards equal rights for women

Muslims believe that God created men and women equally:

All people are equal…as the teeth of a comb. (Hadith)

Traditional male roles
- Protect women and children
- Provide for their wives and children
- Go to the mosque for prayer
- Inherit property

Traditional female roles
- A woman is, most importantly, a wife and mother
- Look after the home and the family
- Do not have to go to the mosque for prayer
- Inherit only half of what a man can

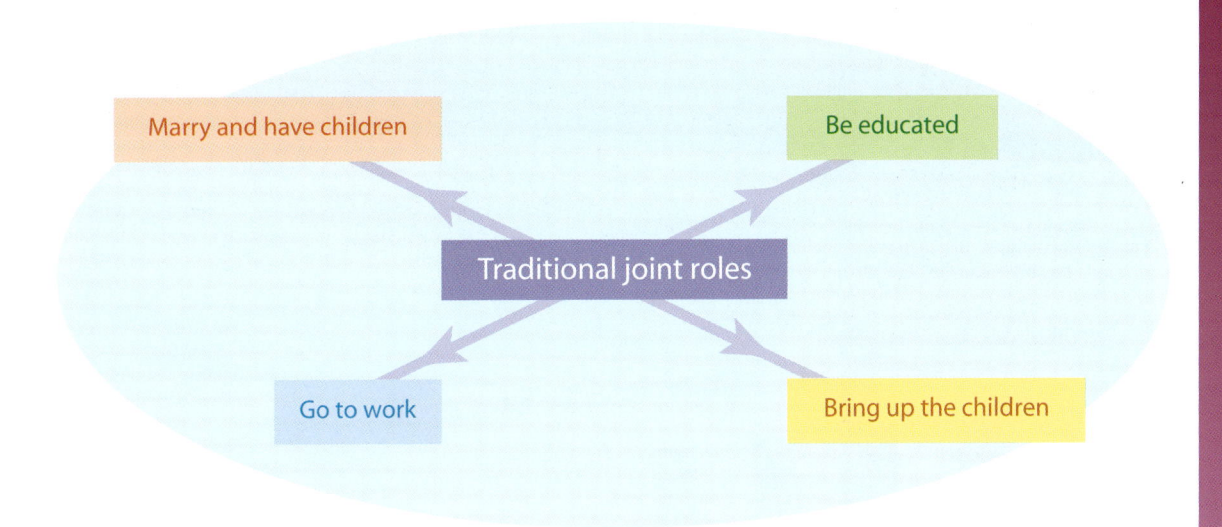

Diagram: **Traditional joint roles** — Marry and have children; Be educated; Go to work; Bring up the children.

Religious inequality

Muslim families pray together at home but in the mosque men and women are separated. Many women object to this, claiming that, in the early days of Islam, men and women worshipped together and there were female leaders. The Hadith (sayings of the Prophet) says:

The search for knowledge is a duty of every Muslim, male or female.

Social inequality

Muslim women may go out to work but are also entitled to expect their husband to provide for them, even if the woman herself is wealthy. However, women can inherit only half as much as men, because they have the financial responsibility to provide for the family. The inheritance provisions are called 'a degree of advantage'.

Both men and women are required to dress modestly. The holy book of Islam, the Qur'an, states:

Women have the same rights in relation to their husbands as are expected in all decency of them ... (Surah 2:228)

Traditionally, men must wear loose clothing and cover themselves from at least the navel to the knee. In many Muslim countries, women cover their heads and bodies with a 'burqa' which is a full-length, loose-fitting garment designed so that even the outline of a woman's body cannot be seen. Often this is worn with a veil (niqab) to cover the face.

In the UK, many Muslim women wear loose, Western clothing with a scarf known as a 'hijab' to cover their hair and shoulders.

Muslim women in Afghanistan wearing the burqa

Muslim women are divided concerning appearance. Some believe that women should be free to wear whatever they wish and that religious clothing can cause prejudice and ill-feeling. However, other women say that wearing religious clothing gives them some privacy from stares and is a symbol of their Islamic faith. The Qur'an says:

Tell thy wives and thy daughters…to draw their cloaks around them. That will be better, so that they may be recognised and not annoyed. Allah is ever forgiving, merciful. (Surah 33:59)

Test yourself

1. List in two columns the ways in which men and women in Islam are treated with both equality and inequality.

2. Suggest **three** problems that have arisen from inequality in Islam and the possible solutions to these problems.

3. What is the meaning of the following quotations:

   'All people are equal…as the teeth of a comb' (Hadith).

   'The search for knowledge is a duty of every Muslim, male or female.'

   'Women have the same rights in relation to their husbands as are expected in all decency of them.'

4. With reference to the each of the following statements, state whether you agree, giving your reasons and showing that you have considered other points of view:

   'Men and women should be allowed to wear whatever they wish.'

   'Islam does little to discourage sexist attitudes.'

   'A wealthy Muslim woman should not expect her husband to keep her.'

Examination question

a **What is religious equality?** (2 marks)

b **Do you think that Islam is sexist? Give two reasons for your view.** (6 marks)

c **Why do some Muslim women support the idea of wearing religious clothing and others do not?** (8 marks)

d **'Men and women should be allowed to worship together as equals.'**
   i **Do you agree? Give reasons for your view.** (3 marks)
   ii **Give reasons why some people may disagree with you.** (3 marks)

Exam tip

Remember that, when answering a question, this is about Muslim attitudes to the role of women, which is different from contrasting the roles of men and women — it's a common mistake.

Topic 30
The UK as a multi-ethnic society

The UK is a multi-ethnic country. This means that many different races, cultures and nationalities live together peacefully in one society. This is called 'ethnic' or '**racial harmony**'. The UK became a **multi-ethnic society** after the Second World War, when people were offered asylum to prevent them from being persecuted abroad. Later, as the countries of the former British empire gained their independence, many people from those countries came to live and work in the UK.

The 2001 census showed that UK society looked like this, with the following ethnic groups:

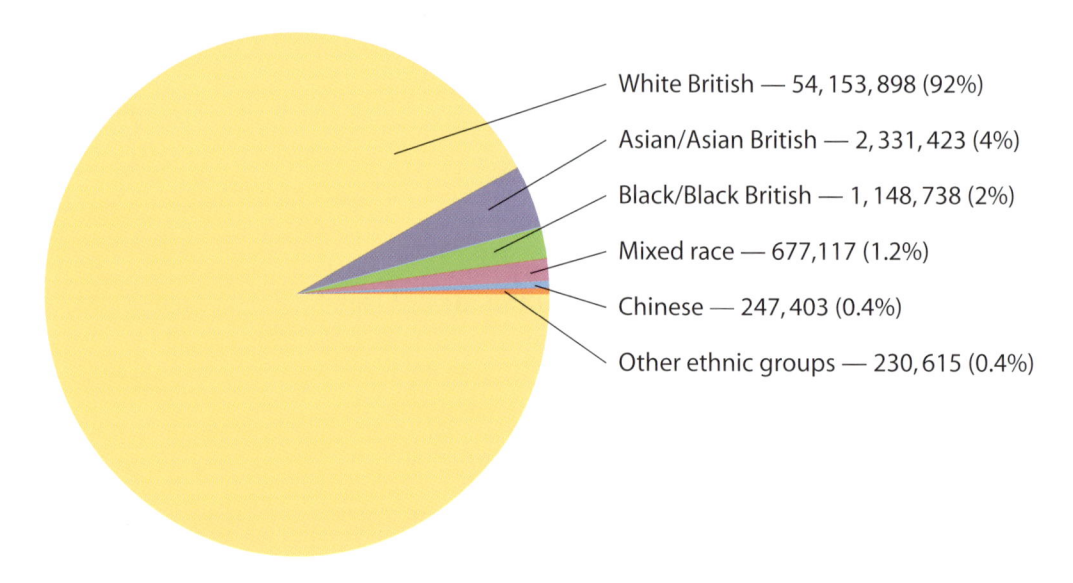

- White British — 54,153,898 (92%)
- Asian/Asian British — 2,331,423 (4%)
- Black/Black British — 1,148,738 (2%)
- Mixed race — 677,117 (1.2%)
- Chinese — 247,403 (0.4%)
- Other ethnic groups — 230,615 (0.4%)

There are many advantages to living in a multi-ethnic society:
- It helps people of different races and cultures to understand and appreciate one another.
- It enables people to understand different religions and beliefs.
- It gives everyone access to a wider variety of music, food, clothes and culture.
- It can bring new people with fresh ideas.
- It makes people more tolerant of the beliefs and feelings of others.

However, living in a multi-ethnic society can have disadvantages:
- Some people can feel scared of cultures that they do not understand.
- Some people are worried that immigrants will take their jobs and homes.

- Some people adopt **racist** views.
- Some people display feelings of **prejudice** and **discrimination.**
- Some think that British culture is vanishing or being replaced by foreign culture.
- There have been some violent clashes between different racial and ethnic groups.

Key words

Discrimination — treating people less favourably; racial discrimination does this because of their race, colour or ethnic origin

Multi-ethnic society — where many different races and cultures live together in one society

Prejudice — judging people as inferior or superior on the basis of, for example, their race or gender

Racial harmony — people of different races living in peace together

Racism — believing that some races are superior to others

The annual Notting Hill Carnival in London demonstrates Britain's multi-ethnic and multi-racial society

Test yourself

1. Explain the meaning of the following terms:
   - multi-ethnic society
   - prejudice
   - discrimination
   - racism
   - racial harmony

2. In two columns, list the advantages and disadvantages of the UK as a multi-ethnic society.

3. Identify **four** features of UK society that show its multi-ethnic nature.

4. Suggest **three** social problems that have arisen from racism, and possible solutions to these problems.

Examination question

a What is a multi-ethnic society? *(2 marks)*

b Do you think that there should be tougher laws against ethnic and racial discrimination in the UK? Give two reasons for your view. *(6 marks)*

c Why do some people support the idea of a multi-ethnic society and others do not? *(8 marks)*

d 'The advantages of living in a multi-cultural society far outweigh the disadvantages.'
   i Do you agree? Give reasons for your view. *(3 marks)*
   ii Give reasons why some people may disagree with you. *(3 marks)*

Exam tip
Racism and stirring up racial/ethnic hatred are offences in the UK.

Topic 31
Government action to promote community cohesion

- with a sense of belonging
- appreciating and valuing the differences between people of different cultures
- Community cohesion means different communities living together…
- with equal opportunities for all in the community
- having good relationships with people of different races

However, **community cohesion** is not easy to achieve and, over the years, the UK government has had to take action to promote community cohesion and to ensure that people of all races and backgrounds live together peacefully.

The major problem — racial discrimination in the UK

In the 1950s and 1960s, thousands of people, mainly from the West Indies, India and Pakistan, immigrated to the UK in search of work and a better standard of living. This caused tension and anger among many people who were already living in the UK. This led to feelings of racism among some people for the following reasons:
- fear that immigrants would take their jobs and houses
- fear that immigrants would take over the local community

This led to racial discrimination, where many of the immigrants were treated less favourably because of their racial or ethnic origins and ended up with the worst jobs and houses in the poorest areas.

Many immigrants ended up in housing in the poorest areas of the UK

Government action to combat racial discrimination

In the 1970s the UK government took the following actions:
- The Race Relations Act 1976 made it unlawful to discriminate because of race, colour, ethnic or national origin in employment, housing, education or healthcare.
- It became illegal to use language likely to stir up racial hatred.
- The Commission for Racial Equality was set up to fight issues of racism.

More recently, and in order to help young people and local ethnic communities, the government has set up:
- the Community Facilitation Programme
- Neighbourhood Renewal Units with the aim of ensuring that local ethnic communities are able to improve the quality of life for those living in the most disadvantaged areas by tackling:
  - poor job prospects
  - high crime levels
  - educational under-achievement
  - poor health
  - problems with housing and their local environment

Community cohesion today

The UK has come a long way and inter-racial and ethnic relationships are much better than they were in the past. However, there is still much to be done because:
- In the UK 74% of all children of Asian origin and 63% of all children of black African origin live in poverty.

- People are concerned about illegal immigrants coming to the UK from Eastern European and other countries.

> **Key words**
>
> **Community cohesion** — where groups of people of different races and ethnic backgrounds live peacefully together in a common framework and set of values

Test yourself

1 Explain the meaning of the following terms:
  - equality
  - racial discrimination
  - ethnic minority
  - community cohesion

2 Suggest **three** reasons why racial discrimination occurred in the UK in the 1950s and 1960s.

3 Identify **two** ways in which the UK government has tried to promote community cohesion.

4 With reference to the each of the following statements, state whether you agree, giving your reasons and showing that you have considered other points of view:

'Laws against racism will never be enough to change racist attitudes.'

'The advantages of living in a multi-cultural society far outweigh the disadvantages.'

'People should have the right to live in whatever country they wish to.'

'All immigrants to the UK should be required to speak English and swear allegiance to the Queen.'

Examination question

a **What is community cohesion?** (2 marks)

b **Do you think that there is still racial discrimination in the UK? Give two reasons for your view.** (6 marks)

c **Why do some people support the idea of community cohesion and others do not?** (8 marks)

d **'Passing laws against racial discrimination will not stop racist feelings.'**
  i **Do you agree? Give reasons for your view.** (3 marks)
  ii **Give reasons why some people may disagree with you.** (3 marks)

Exam tip

In your answers try to consider how living in the UK has changed as a result of large-scale immigration.

Topic 32
Why Christians should promote racial harmony

Biblical teaching

Christians are opposed to racism. The Bible teaches that all races are equal and that Christians should seek racial harmony among all people. Jesus Christ himself treated everyone as equal and, in the Parable of the Good Samaritan (Luke 10:25–37), he taught that people of different races and ethnic groups should not hate each other, but should follow God's command to love one another.

The Bible says…

- 'For God created humankind in his own image' (Genesis 1:27)
- 'As I have loved you, so you must love one another' (John 13:35)
- 'There is neither Jew nor Greek…you are all one in Christ' (Galatians 3:29)
- 'Love your neighbour as yourself' (Luke 10:27)
- 'God shows no partiality but in every nation anyone…is acceptable to him' (Acts 10:34–35)

Martin Luther King (1929–1968)

One famous Christian who worked for racial harmony was Dr Martin Luther King. He believed that God was on the side of the poor and he spent his life campaigning for racial harmony and equal rights for black people in the USA. He led peaceful protests that had the support of thousands of people of all races, trying to convince the government to grant equality to all people. His most famous speech was:

I have a dream that my four little children will one day live in a nation where they will be judged not by the colour of their skin, but by the sort of people they are.

In 1964 he won the Nobel Peace Prize and the following year black people in the USA were given equal voting rights with whites. However, some white racist groups saw him as a threat and he was assassinated by James Earl Ray in 1968.

Martin Luther King Jr

Christianity and racial harmony today

Christians all over the world can be seen working for racial harmony and the Christian churches condemn racism and encourage all Christians to treat everyone equally.

We affirm that racism is a direct contradiction of the gospel of Jesus. (Methodist Church)

Every form of social and cultural discrimination must be curbed and eradicated as incompatible with God's design. (Catechism of the Catholic Church)

Archbishop Desmond Tutu

In recent times, Archbishop Desmond Tutu, the first black Archbishop of South Africa, has encouraged Christians by working tirelessly for racial harmony. He has been imprisoned for his beliefs many times but, through peaceful protests, he was able, in 1994, to lead a campaign that resulted in equality for black people during the time of white rule in South Africa. Desmond Tutu said that the inspiration for his work was the teaching of Jesus. He constantly encouraged people of all races to join together and to forgive one another. He said:

If it were not for faith, I am certain that lots of us would be hate-filled and bitter…but to speak of God, you must speak of your neighbour.

Today in the UK, the Christian churches try to encourage racial harmony through the work of specialist groups such as:
- The Race and Community Relations Committee, which advises Christians on issues of racism.
- The Committee on Black Anglican Concerns, which helps Christian organisations to develop anti-racist campaigns.

Test yourself

1 Outline the meaning of the following quotations and consider one problem that may be raised by each of them:

'God created humankind in his own image...male and female, he created them' (Genesis 1: 27).

'There is neither Jew nor Greek, slave nor free, male nor female, for you are all one in Christ' (Galatians 3:28).

'God does not show favouritism, but accepts people from every nation' (Acts 10:34–35).

'Love your neighbour as yourself' (Luke 10:27).

2 Suggest **three** social problems that have arisen from racism, and give possible solutions to these problems.

3 Identify **three** features of UK life that show that it has racial harmony.

4 In what ways has the work of (i) Martin Luther King and (ii) Archbishop Desmond Tutu been so important?

Examination question

a **What is racial harmony?** (2 marks)

b **Do you think that there is racial harmony in the UK? Give two reasons for your view.** (6 marks)

c **Why do some people feel that the work of Martin Luther King and Desmond Tutu was very successful and others do not?** (8 marks)

d **'The Christian Church has not done enough to fight racism.'**
   i Do you agree? Give reasons for your view. (3 marks)
   ii Give reasons why some people may disagree with you. (3 marks)

Exam tip

Remember that this unit is about Christians, so try to include relevant biblical material and quotations to support your answers.

Topic 33
Why Muslims should promote racial harmony

Islam supports racial harmony and every Muslim is part of the ummah — the community of Muslims worldwide. All Muslims, irrespective of their race or colour, are united by their religious faith. Today, there are Muslims from many races, showing that, in Islam, all races are equal.

Islamic teaching on racial harmony

- the message of the Qur'an is for all people of every race
- in the same speech, the Prophet said: 'People descend from Adam, and Adam was made out of dust'
- 'O humanity, I am the messenger of God to you all!' (Surah 7:158)

The Qur'an and the Prophet teach…

- the only thing that distinguishes one human being from another is their good or bad actions
- 'There is no superiority for an Arab over a non-Arab, neither for a white man over a black man…' (The Farewell Pilgrimage Speech of the Prophet)

Muslims show their unity and harmony in the following ways:
- Muslims all pray together in Arabic.
- All pray facing the qibla of Makkah.
- Muslims from all over the world make the pilgrimage (Hajj) to the holy city.
- In the month of Ramada, all Muslims join together in fasting and feasting.

Muslims on Hajj in the holy city

Malcolm X (1925–1965)

One of the most famous Muslim campaigners for racial equality and harmony was Malcolm X (El-Hajj Malik El-Shabazz). After an early life of crime, Malcolm X joined a radical Muslim religious organisation, the Nation of Islam, which taught that white people were preventing black people from achieving any success. The Nation of Islam campaigned for a separate country of its own with only black citizens living in it. Malcolm X became a minister for the Nation of Islam and spread the message through TV and radio shows.

Malcolm X believed that the greatest example of racial harmony was the Hajj and he declared:

There were tens of thousands of pilgrims from all over the world…But we were all participating in the same ritual, displaying a spirit of unity and brotherhood that my experiences in America had led me to believe could not exist between the white and non-white.

In 1964, Malcolm X left the Nation of Islam and founded the Muslim Mosque, which campaigned for racial harmony in the USA. His most famous speech was:

I am not a racist. I am against every form of racism and segregation, every form of discrimination. I believe in human beings and that all human beings should be respected as such, regardless of their colour.

Some people were worried by what he said, for he sometimes seemed to suggest that change might come only after a violent struggle. Malcolm X had a huge following, but he was a very controversial figure. In 1965 he was assassinated by members of the Nation of Islam.

Test yourself

1 Outline the meaning of the following quotations and consider one problem that may be raised by each of them:

'O humanity, I am the messenger of God to you all!' (Surah 7:158)

'There is no superiority for an Arab over a non-Arab, neither for a white man over a black man…'

'People descend from Adam, and Adam was made out of dust.'

2 In what ways do Muslims display racial harmony?

3 Identify the different approaches to racial harmony adopted by Muslims and Christians. Which is the more effective and why?

4 Compare the life and work of Martin Luther King and Malcolm X. Who do you think was the more successful and why? Give reasons.

5 Do you think Muslims are more concerned with religious harmony than with racial harmony?

Examination question

a **What is racism?** (2 marks)

b **Do you think that there will ever be racial harmony in the world? Give two reasons for your view.** (6 marks)

c **Why do some people feel that the work of Malcolm X was very successful and others do not?** (8 marks)

d **'Religion does not help racial harmony.'**
   i **Do you agree? Give reasons for your view.** (3 marks)
   ii **Give reasons why some people may disagree with you.** (3 marks)

Exam tip
Remember that this unit is about Muslim attitudes, so try to include relevant Islamic material and quotations to support your answers.

Topic 34
The UK as a multi-faith society

The UK is made up of people of many different religious beliefs. There are several religious groups in the UK. Of the main religious groups, there are approximately:

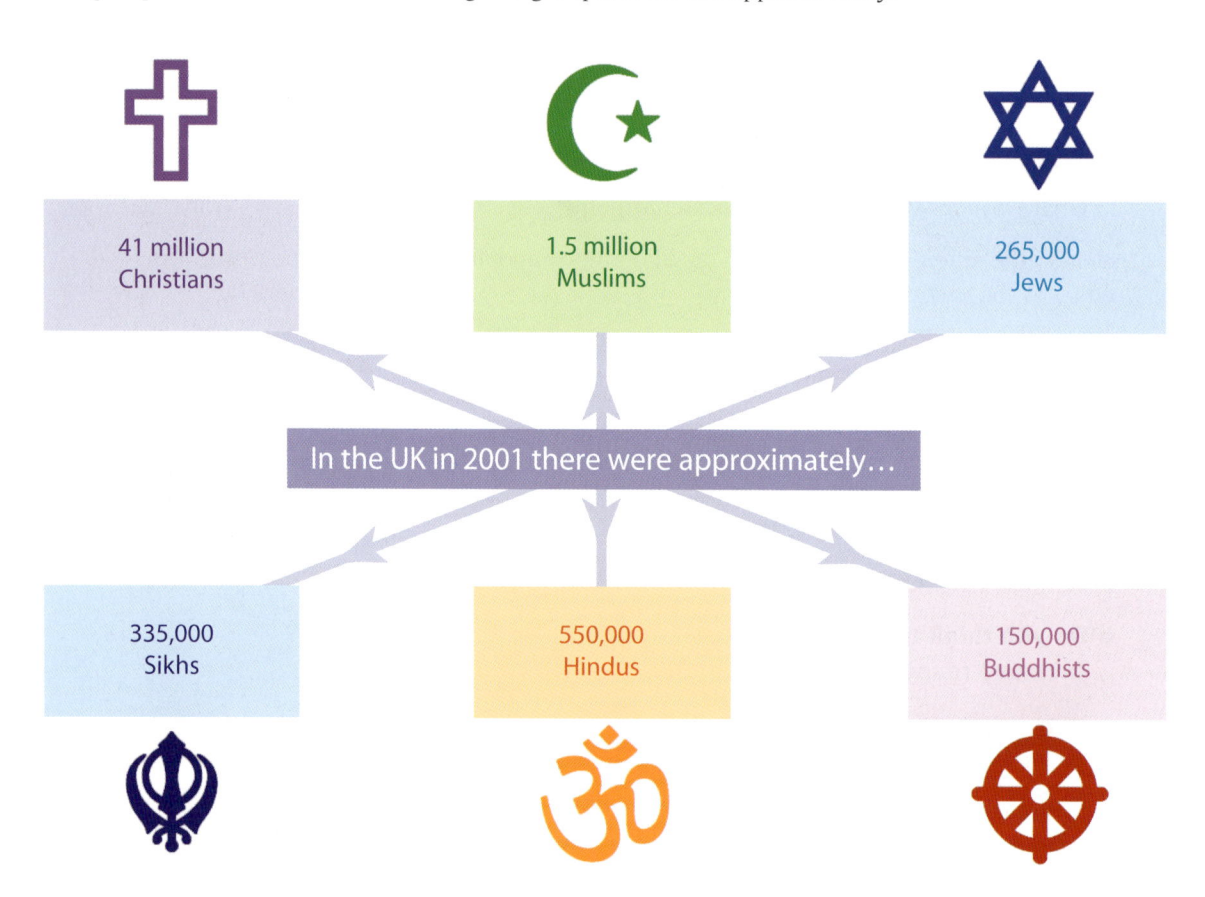

In the UK in 2001 there were approximately…

- 41 million Christians
- 1.5 million Muslims
- 265,000 Jews
- 335,000 Sikhs
- 550,000 Hindus
- 150,000 Buddhists

Today, the UK:
- is a **multi-faith society** where people of different religious faiths live peacefully together
- offers **religious pluralism** — all religions have an equal right to co-exist
- offers **religious freedom** — members of all religions are free to worship

Religion and community cohesion

A multi-faith service in Trafalgar Square, London

Key words

Multi-faith society — where many different religious groups live together in one society

Religious freedom — people are free to practise their religion

Religious pluralism — where all religions have the equal right to co-exist

Religious Studies 109

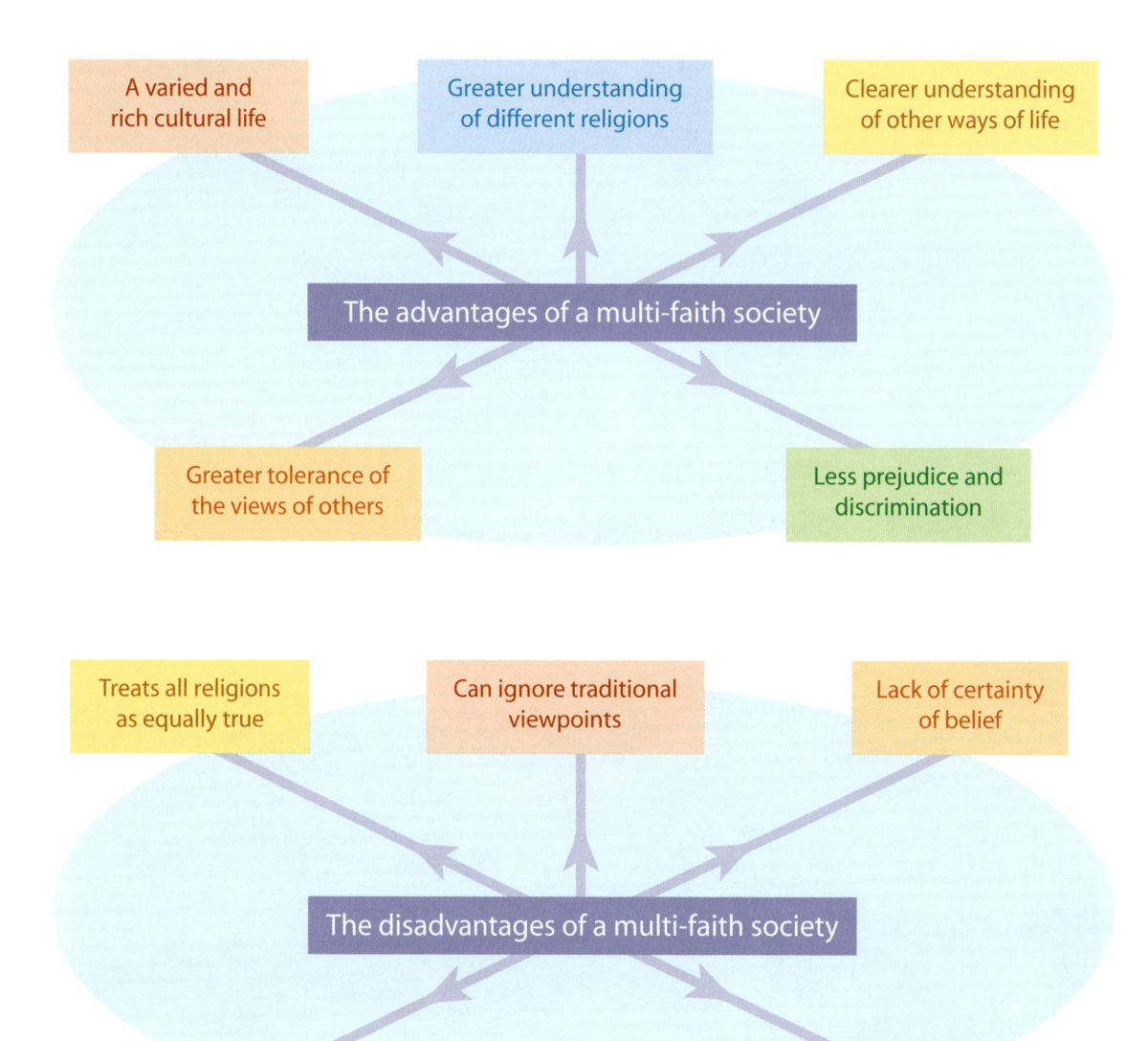

The advantages of a multi-faith society

- A varied and rich cultural life
- Greater understanding of different religions
- Clearer understanding of other ways of life
- Greater tolerance of the views of others
- Less prejudice and discrimination

The disadvantages of a multi-faith society

- Treats all religions as equally true
- Can ignore traditional viewpoints
- Lack of certainty of belief
- Different moral viewpoints
- Makes some people feel threatened

Test yourself

1. Explain the meaning of the following terms:
   - multi-ethnic society
   - multi-faith society
   - religious freedom

2. In two columns, list all the advantages and disadvantages of living in a multi-faith society. What, do you think, is the greatest advantage/disadvantage?

3. Identify **three** features of UK society that show its multi-faith nature.

Examination question

a What is a multi-faith society? *(2 marks)*

b Do you think that all religions are equally valid? Give two reasons for your view. *(6 marks)*

c Why do some people feel that living in a multi-faith society is a good thing and others do not? *(8 marks)*

d 'The advantages of living in a multi-faith society outweigh the disadvantages.'
  i Do you agree? Give reasons for your view. *(3 marks)*
  ii Give reasons why some people may disagree with you. *(3 marks)*

Exam tip

This unit is about the UK as a multi-faith society. Concentrate on the advantages and disadvantages this brings, so try to include relevant material, including statistics, to support your answers.

Topic 35
Issues raised about multi-faith societies

Are all faiths equally true?

One of the biggest issues about living in a multi-faith society is the question of whether all religious faiths are equally valid and true. Some religious believers in the UK say that people should be allowed the religious freedom to follow whatever religion they like, or none. However, others say that only their religion is right and that everyone should follow it.

Inclusivism
Only one religion is completely right and the other religions, although they may help someone to God, are not fully right. These religions should be respected, but their followers may be encouraged to change to the 'right' faith

Three different viewpoints

Pluralism
There are many different religions that lead to God and people should be free to follow whichever one they wish, or to follow none at all

Exclusivism
Only one religion is right and all the others are wrong; members of the right faith should seek to convert all others to their faith

Some Christians are exclusivist and believe that Christianity is the only true faith. They believe that it is their duty to try to convert all people to Christianity. This view has some support from the Church and the Bible:

The Church still has the obligation and also the sacred right to evangelise all men.
(*Catechism of the Catholic Church*)

Jesus said 'I am the way and the truth and the life. No one comes to the father except through me.' (John 14:6)

Other Christians are inclusivist and say that, while Christianity has the complete truth, other religions have part of the truth and should be allowed to continue their search for God.

The Catholic Church recognises in other religions that search for the God who is unknown yet near. (*Catechism of the Catholic Church*)

Multi-faith problems arising in the UK

Problems have arisen from the multi-faith nature of society in the UK:
- There have been a number of violent clashes between members of different faiths.
- Some people say that the UK is a Christian country, not a multi-faith one, and that Christian traditions should have priority.
- Some members of non-Christian faiths say that too much emphasis is placed on Christianity.

A Winter Light festival has replaced traditional Christian nativity scenes in some English towns

The advantages and disadvantages of interfaith marriages

A particular problem can arise in **interfaith (multi-faith) marriages**. In some religions, married couples are required to be of the same faith and sometimes parents arrange marriages for their grown-up children. This can cause serious problems because young people who have lived all their lives in the UK may want to choose a marriage partner for themselves — even a partner who is not from their own faith. This can be a source of conflict in many religious families.

Even after a couple from different faiths get married, there can still be important decisions to be made. For instance, the couple must decide:

- what religion their children will belong to
- how their children will be raised
- which religious festivals they will observe
- which religious community the family will belong to

> **Key words**
>
> **Interfaith marriages** — where two people from different religions marry each other
>
> **Religious exclusivism** — only one religion is right and all the others are wrong
>
> **Religious inclusivism** — one religion is completely right and the other religions have only part of the truth

Test yourself

1 Explain the meaning of the following terms:
   - religious pluralism
   - religious freedom
   - religious inclusivism
   - religious exclusivism

2 Using two columns, list how (i) Christians and (ii) Muslims might argue that their faith is the only true one.

3 Should members of religious faiths try to covert others to their faith?

4 Suggest **three** arguments in favour of interfaith marriages, and three arguments against.

5 Suggest **three** social problems that have arisen from the UK being a multi-faith society and possible solutions to these problems.

6 With reference to the each of the following statements, identify the problems that arise from them and how they might be resolved:

'It is the duty of all believers to convert others to their faith.'

Jesus said 'I am the way and the truth and the life. No one comes to the father except through me' (John 14:6).

'The Catholic Church recognises in other religions that search for the God who is unknown yet near' (*Catechism of the Catholic Church*).

'Islam is the only true faith.'

'There can be no such thing as one true faith — all religions offer a chance to reach God.'

Examination question

a What is an interfaith marriage? (2 marks)

b Do you think that there is only one true faith? Give two reasons for your view. (6 marks)

c Why do some people feel that the UK is a multi-faith society and others do not? (8 marks)

d 'It is right for parents to choose marriage partners for their children — parents know best.'
  i Do you agree? Give reasons for your view. (3 marks)
  ii Give reasons why some people may disagree with you. (3 marks)

Exam tip

This unit is about the problems of living in a multi-faith society. Concentrate on the main problems and try to think of possible solutions. Use relevant background material to support your answers.

Topic 36
Ways in which religions work to promote community cohesion

All religions want to have a world in which everyone lives in peace together, regardless of their religious faith. However, for members of different religions, living together can be quite challenging and they have to work hard to promote friendship and community cohesion.

To promote community cohesion among people of different races and faiths, people have to…

- share common values such as tolerance, respect, charity and non-violence
- be prepared to listen to each other's views
- learn to live and work together
- respect each other's religious faith

Groups working for cohesion

The Council of Christians and Jews/ The Inter-faith Network for the United Kingdom

These two groups have been working together in recent years to solve problems and bring harmony to people of different faiths. The former is particularly concerned with relations between Jews and Christians and the latter promotes dialogue and discussion between a wide range of faiths and organisations. Both groups work supporting the view that God created all people to have a relationship with him.

Another way in which community cohesion is achieved is where people of different faiths share their festivals together. However, this has caused problems. For example, some people have complained that certain city councils believe that celebrating Christmas in a public way may be offensive to non-Christians and are refusing to put up Christmas signs and instead are calling it a 'Winter Festival'. Those opposed to this say that it excludes Christianity.

Going further, some religious groups suggest that the way to community cohesion is to recognise that all religions are equal and should become one world faith and that terms such as 'Christian' and 'Muslim' should no longer be used.

The annual Bradford Mela — a cultural festival held by the city council for the Muslim and Hindu communities in the area

The Muslim Council of Britain

The Muslim Council works to promote community cohesion by building strong communities who can give mutual support to those in need. It also encourages Muslims to take an active part in UK society rather than living just with other Muslims in isolated communities.

The Council is also active in the social sphere, having campaigned for the police to treat Muslim youths more fairly. It has also requested that the government places more Muslims in high-ranking jobs, for instance, in the police, in order to promote a good Muslim role model.

Problems can, however, arise when religious groups fail to understand one another. For instance, in 2006, Cabinet Minister Jack Straw caused an outcry when he suggested that Muslim women wearing the veil were causing a barrier to community cohesion because it was difficult to make conversation with them while they were wearing the veil.

Faith schools

Faith schools may also aid community cohesion. These are schools run on religious lines. In the UK there are 6,580 Christian-based schools, with 37 Jewish schools, 7 Islamic and 2 Sikh. Having schools of different faiths is said to improve educational standards and understanding among the various religious communities. However, opponents of faith schools claim that they are exclusive to that religion and do not give their pupils a fair understanding of other faiths.

Jack Straw

A Muslim woman wearing the veil

Test yourself

1. In two columns, list the beliefs and values of Christianity and Islam. Which beliefs are similar and which are different? Why do you think this is?
2. Do you think that Christmas should be a holiday for everyone in the UK or is it offensive to other religions? Give reasons for your view.
3. In what other ways may following a particular religious faith cause problems for community cohesion in a multi-faith society?
4. Identify **three** ways in which religious organisations seek to promote community cohesion in the UK.

Examination question

a What is tolerance? (2 marks)

b Do you think that all religions should join together as one world faith? Give two reasons for your view. (6 marks)

c Why do some people feel that the government should do more to promote community cohesion and others do not? (8 marks)

d 'Faith schools hinder, rather than help community cohesion.'
   i Do you agree? Give reasons for your view. (3 marks)
   ii Give reasons why some people may disagree with you. (3 marks)

Exam tip

This unit is about religious groups working for community cohesion. Concentrate on how successful or otherwise these efforts are. Look at the issue of how much community cohesion there actually is in the UK.

Topic 37
Issues of religion and community cohesion in the media

Soaps

Many television programmes use themes concerning religious or community cohesion issues in their most moving and interesting storylines. For example, in the soaps there have been the following stories:

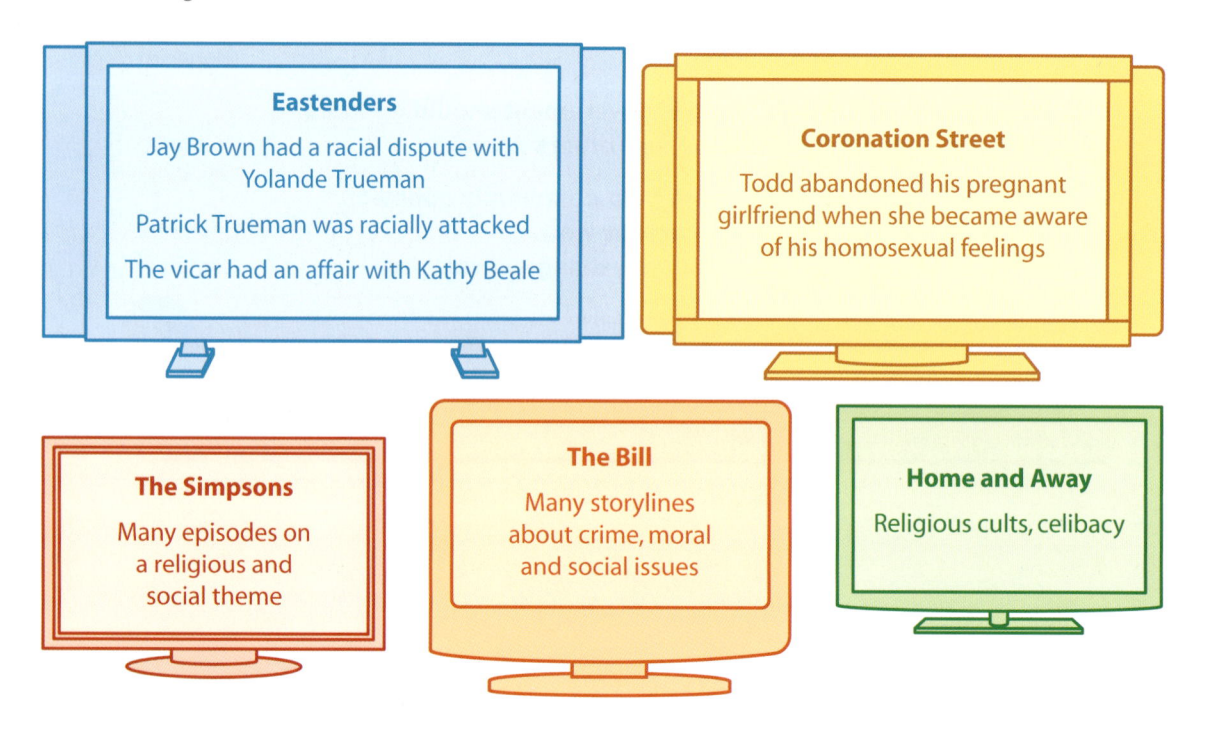

Eastenders
Jay Brown had a racial dispute with Yolande Trueman
Patrick Trueman was racially attacked
The vicar had an affair with Kathy Beale

Coronation Street
Todd abandoned his pregnant girlfriend when she became aware of his homosexual feelings

The Simpsons
Many episodes on a religious and social theme

The Bill
Many storylines about crime, moral and social issues

Home and Away
Religious cults, celibacy

There are also television documentaries and factual programmes, such as *Panorama*, that examine controversial issues such as abortion, euthanasia and race relations. Similarly, on radio, programmes such as *The Moral Maze* and one-off documentaries deal with religious and community themes.

Indeed, a serious racial controversy arose in *Celebrity Big Brother*. In January 2007, Jade Goody was evicted from the house after she made allegedly racist remarks to another contestant, Shilpa Shetty, whom she referred to as 'Shilpa Poppadom'.

Jade Goody and Shilpa Shetty

One of the biggest problems facing the media over issues of religion and community cohesion concerns newspapers. Occasionally, editors receive complaints that what they write is only one side of the argument or that they fail to give the viewers a balanced view of what is really happening.

Another problem is that of the internet and, in particular, the way some extremist groups are able to pass their views to a very wide, often young, audience.

Test yourself

1. List all the religious and community cohesion storylines you can think of that have appeared in soaps or other television dramas. How well or badly do you think they tackled these issues?

2. Do you ever watch television documentaries or listen to radio programmes about religious or community cohesion issues? Why or why not? Give reasons.

3. Examine the way in which a religious or moral issue has been tackled in a film you have seen.

4 Examine the meaning of the following quotations. Do you agree or disagree with them? Give reasons.

'Television programmes never take religious believers seriously.'

'The media can distort the truth.'

'In a multi-faith society, there should be no religious broadcasting.'

'It was right to expel Jade Goody from Celebrity Big Brother.'

'Religious broadcasting makes a positive contribution to multi-cultural Britain.'

Examination question

a What is the media? *(2 marks)*

b Do you think that the UK needs more or less religious and community broadcasting? Give two reasons for your view. *(6 marks)*

c Why do some people feel that the internet is a good thing for social harmony and others do not? *(8 marks)*

d 'The media is always biased against religion.'
   i Do you agree? Give reasons for your view. *(3 marks)*
   ii Give reasons why some people may disagree with you. *(3 marks)*

Exam tip
This unit is about the treatment of racial and community cohesion issues in the UK. Concentrate on a range of media styles — television, radio, newspapers and internet. Consider the advantages and disadvantages each brings and include relevant examples to support your answers.

Key word index

abortion 44
adultery 61
aesthetic argument 24
agnostic 8
Akhira 38
analogy 19
antitheist 8
assisted suicide 50
atheist 8
baptism 10
Bible 10
big bang theory 21
causation 18
celibacy 76
civil partnerships 59
cohabitation 58
community cohesion 99
confession of sins 16
confirmation 10
contraception 80
conversion 12
design 18
discrimination 97
divorce 59
equality 87

euthanasia 50
evolution 21
faithfulness 61
homosexuality 59
immortality of the soul 37
initiation ceremony 10
intelligent design 25
intercession 16
interfaith marriages 114
Janannam 39
Jannat 39
meditation 16
miracle 14
moral evil 29
multi-ethnic society 96
multi-faith society 108
natural evil 30
natural selection 21
near-death experience 41
non-voluntary euthanasia 50
nuclear family 71
numinous 13
omni-benevolent 8
omnipotent 8

omniscient 8
paranormal 41
petitions 16
prayer 10
prejudice 97
pre-marital sex 61
procreation 70
promiscuity 61
quality of life 52
racial harmony 96
racism 97
re-constituted family 71
religious exclusivism 112
religious freedom 108
religious inclusivism 112
religious pluralism 108
re-marriage 66
resurrection of the body 38
sanctity of life 46
sexism 87
testimony 10
thanksgiving 16
theist 8
voluntary euthanasia 50
worship 16